Reading as Collective Action

texts as tactics

Nicholas Hengen Fox

University of Iowa Press Iowa City

University of Iowa Press, Iowa City 52242

www.uipress.uiowa.edu
Printed in the United States of America

Design by Omega Clay

The University of Iowa Press is a member of Green Press Initiative and is committed to preserving natural resources.

Printed on acid-free paper

Library of Congress Cataloging-in-Publication Data

Names: Fox, Nicholas Hengen author.
Title: Reading as collective action : texts as tactics / Nicholas Hengen Fox.
Description: Iowa City : University of Iowa Press, 2017. | Includes bibliographical references and index.
Identifiers: LCCN 2017005566 | ISBN 9781609385255 (pbk) | ISBN 9781609385262 (ebk)
Subjects: LCSH: Books and reading—United States. | Literature and Society—United States. | American literature—20th century—History and criticism.
Classification: LCC Z1003.2 .F69 2017 | DDC 028/.9—dc23
LC record available at https://lccn.loc.gov/2017005566

August, 2018

Reading as Collective Action

For Alan from
Sheila & Larry Teplin...
Over the years, you
have helped all of us
so much! Our
son-in-law Nic (married
to our youngest daughter,
Emily) wrote this book.
He is a college professor
in Portland, Oregon.

[illegible]

For Nathaniel,

his friends,

and the better world

they deserve

Contents

Acknowledgments ix

PROLOGUE

Blueprints 1

1 Dissent after September 11
How Poetry Reclaims Human Rights 8

2 *The Grapes of Wrath* and the Great Recession
Literature Gets People What They Need 34

3 Talking with Strangers about Working-Class Literature
Against Service Learning 61

4 Reconnecting the Political
Tactics, Literary Studies, and Publicly Engaged Scholarship 84

EPILOGUE

Building a Better World 108

Notes 111

Bibliography 137

Index 149

Acknowledgments

I am lucky to be able to pause here—after ten years at work on this project—and acknowledge a few particularly deep sources of support. Tim Brennan, a generous adviser still, taught me to be a grounded materialist—and to show my work. Kevin Riordan, who read every word here (some of them many times), provided a model of sympathetic criticism I can only hope to emulate. My reading and thinking were forged by Rita Felski and Jerry McGann at Virginia; at Minnesota by Paula Rabinowitz, Maria Damon, and Eric Daigre. I hope this book does these generous guides proud.

A shout-out, too, to my fellow Emaciated Gophers at Minnesota and my Social Justice Focus Award collaborators—faculty, staff, and students—at PCC. You have offered powerful fuel for this project.

My thanks are due to many editors whose labors shaped sentences, paragraphs, and ideas: Rita Felski (again) at *New Literary History*; Linda Dittmar and Frinde Maher at *Radical Teacher*; Catherine Cocks (and everyone) at the University of Iowa Press. My gratitude also to the *many* anonymous reviewers, who challenged my ideas and helped me develop, clarify, and focus. I hope they will see the value of their labors here.

The graduate school at the University of Minnesota provided essential funding: a doctoral dissertation fellowship and a Graduate Research Partnership Program summer stipend underwrote the second chapter. The Department of English also awarded me the Audrey Christensen Award, which allowed me to write in the margins of many of my own books. Thanks to both English at Minnesota and my current Arts and English division at PCC, who have funded my travel to conferences where I worked out versions of these chapters, as well.

A decade is an awfully long time to live with any project—especially one that must've appeared, to put it gently, quixotic. Emily, you kept listening, kept helping me puzzle through, and never told me to stop. Your support is—I mean this literally—beyond comprehension; I'm beyond grateful for it and for you.

Prologue

blueprints

Literature is powerful. It offers respite. It provides access to beauty and horror, to new places, new people, and new ideas. It can, as the phrase goes, change your life. Good things, all of them. But also somewhat limited goods: they're all pretty passive, pretty private—you might even say self-centered.

Reading as Collective Action shifts our focus outward, to another of literature's powers: the power to reshape, in very public, very active ways, our world. In this book, you will encounter readers who criticized the Bush Administration's War on Terror by republishing poems by writers ranging from Shakespeare to Amiri Baraka everywhere from lampposts to the *New York Times*. You will read about people in Michigan and Tennessee who leveraged a community reading program on John Steinbeck's *The Grapes of Wrath* to organize support for those in need during the Great Recession and to engage with their neighbors about immigration. You will meet a pair of students who took to public transit to talk with strangers about working-class literature and a trio who created a literary website that reclaimed the working-class history of the Pacific Northwest.

These stories showcase the political power unleashed when we read literature in public and collaborative ways. They also provide actionable blueprints. Take them, please, and build something of your own. My hope is that they help you, reader, to connect your reading with our responsibility to create a more just world.

When you read texts as tactics, you don't read to show how smart you are (to, say, get a good grade or scholarly kudos). Attention to *what* texts say and *how* they say it is important, but it's *where* and *to whom* they say it that make them capable of changing things in the world. So reading texts as tactics is a way to work across differences, to connect with others, to develop the political power to make a more just world. As shorthand, I'll often refer to this approach to literature as a kind of "everyday politics." I borrow the phrase from Harry Boyte, an activist (and a scholar), who participates in and studies community-based collaborations in everyday places where everyday people are "co-creator[s] of democracy."[1]

The readers who use texts as tactics work in and around these everyday places—churches, community organizations, streets, and schools. They use reading to bring new language, ideas, and practices from texts into conversations. As one conversation becomes two, tactical readers can shape not only the language used in those spaces, but how those spaces operate. And this isn't insular work: in the hands of tactical readers, books—and conversations about them—build bridges between groups that might never have otherwise spoken. This process develops coalitions around transformative language and ideas, while simultaneously growing organizational capacities to enact broader change. The readers whose stories I tell here use reading to create a more just world—among their fellow readers, in their wider communities, and even at the level of law and governmental structures.

The phrase "everyday politics" captures a wide range of practices, but as I get deeper into these stories I'll develop more technical language to characterize the work of these readers. Tactical readers demand justice. And, as political theorist Nancy Fraser has argued, today "theories of justice must become three-dimensional, incorporating the political dimension of *representation* alongside the economic dimension of *distribution* and the cultural dimension of *recognition*."[2] Tactical readers work on all three aspects. They try to humanize people who are ignored or demeaned; they try to build understandings of those who are marginalized or under attack. To credit literature with the work of recognition is, perhaps, not so surprising. But tactical readers also shape political representation by amplifying marginalized voices within governmental and civic institutions and by empowering them to work against existing power structures as well. More remarkable still, they also engage in redistribution: economic (sharing money); material (sharing food); and immaterial (sharing suppressed knowledge and ideas).

Each chapter develops those definitions as it traces how ideas and practices from books and their readers move through conversations and into concrete actions that create more equitable communities and institutions. Indeed, I'll show how the things that make literature "literature"—shareable narratives, powerful language, new ideas, cultural prestige—are actually the very things that, in the hands of these readers, make it a tool for justice. When we read texts as tactics, "that book changed my life" can become "that book changed *our* lives."

Reading as Collective Action illustrates how literature—in the United States in the early twenty-first century—can be a key player in creating a more just world. The book's first three chapters tell the stories of tactical readers engaged in this work.

Chapter 1, "Dissent after September 11: How Poetry Reclaims Human Rights," examines how literature works as a collective voice for representation in a range of public spheres. I analyze how, in the two months following September 11, 2001, readers read and, as a result of their mass reading, managed to republish poems (as media kept repeating) "everywhere."

These poems—in newspapers and on internet message boards, subway walls, and *The Newshour with Jim Lehrer*—responded to the triumphalist xenophobia that marked the Bush administration's "war on terror." I focus on three widely shared poems written by Sam Hamod, Lorna de Cervantes, and Amiri Baraka, which proved both rhetorically forceful and remarkably difficult to censor. By using these texts as tactics, these (mostly anonymous) readers allowed poems to emphatically voice their political beliefs to a broad public (no small feat in this historic moment) and to organize and encourage diverse audiences to join them in rejecting racial profiling and racist war. Their speech, I argue, wasn't just a call for recognition but active political representation and a reclamation of rights denied to many in those months.

The second chapter, "*The Grapes of Wrath* and the Great Recession: Literature Gets People What They Need," shows how in 2009 readers used *The Grapes of Wrath* (1939) as a means to alleviate local poverty. I visited two communities: Jackson, Michigan, and Knoxville, Tennessee. There I was able to examine how readers participating in the Big Read—a National Endowment for the Arts-sponsored community reading program—used the language, the ideas, and the literary fame of Steinbeck's novel as an organizational tool.

Many readers participated in the program in familiar ways: reading alone or with a few friends in a book club. But tactical readers organized events, like a *Grapes of Wrath*–themed services fair, that became not just a space for literary discussion among a diverse group of people but a place for the delivery of much-needed public services. The book, remarkably, helped people access free meals and advice on escaping foreclosure, among other things. The fair offers a clear example of how people can help each other survive based on models suggested by the novel. As in the first chapter, these tactical readers use literature to garner recognition and political representation; but these tactical readers also use the novel to produce immediate material redistribution.

The third chapter, "Talking with Strangers about Working-Class Literature," describes how, by using texts as tactics, two groups of students took education far beyond the classroom. One group, a pair of young women, orchestrated conversations about working-class literature and culture on public transit; the other, a cross-generational group, produced *Rough Crossing*, a multimedia website that examines working-class experience with an emphasis on the Pacific Northwest. These are practices, again, that encourage recognition (helping make working-class experience visible), representation (bringing working-class voices—both the students' and their literary texts'—into multiple public spheres), and redistribution (in particular the sharing of knowledge the students excavated from archives).

Three very different stories: different people and places, different coalitions and concerns. But they harmonize around a commitment to using literature as a tool for empowering oppressed groups—people in poverty, people of color, immigrants—and around collaborative, public reading practices. Each of these first three chapters shows readers shaping language and ideas, building bridges, and enabling political transformations. They illustrate how to operate tactically: in ways (as Sun Tzu writes) that must shift situationally; in ways that (as Michel de Certeau notes) offer unexpected resistance against (or within) stratified power structures; in ways that ultimately empower readers to make change.[3] And they show what that change looks like.

I gathered these stories as I stumbled along my idiosyncratic academic trajectory. I've moved through sites familiar to literature scholars—seminar rooms, MLA conference panels, and archives where I helped graduate students refine sophisticated research skills. But I've also found myself in less Parnassian venues. In dingy public libraries, I've tutored refugees and people living unhoused; I've buried myself in the spreadsheets of union-organizing drives; I've watched, in improvised classrooms, as brilliant adult learners (rejected by traditional higher education) sat frozen in fear of misreading a poem.

As I moved through graduate school at two research universities and became a tenured faculty member at a community college, I often felt myself unable to reconcile these two worlds. I felt lucky to be at my desk, pursuing my arcane interests within the very real borders that colleges (even open-access institutions) maintain. I felt lucky, in this age of adjunctification, to even have a desk that I could call my own. Still, as I wrote these first three chapters, I was acutely aware of the catastrophic conditions of our larger world—and of how little a traditional academic project would do to improve them.

As I've written this book, though, I've come to see I'm not alone. A growing number of scholars are working hard to make connections, so that academic labors might have a greater impact in the wider world. That only a few of those people are in English departments explains, perhaps, why it took me so long to find the large and growing field of "public engagement." At its best, this approach to teaching, research, and service signifies a deep commitment "to the public purposes of higher education" and a resistance to "the existing policies, structures, and practices that have delegitimized" many of the peoples and ways of knowing that constitute our world.[4] Indeed, this book's first three chapters move through pretty unacademic ways of being and knowing: instead of providing my own close readings of poems, I'm reading what people in newspapers and blogs and e-mails say about them; I'm recounting what community organizers do with *The Grapes of Wrath*, not digging pearls out of the Steinbeck archives. And the work of those tactical readers has helped me develop the empowering teaching strategies that led to *Rough Crossing*.

But this book is also a critique of "civic engagement" (another name often attached to the field), which sometimes seems more a mode of public relations for colleges and universities than a truly transformational field. The final third of the book develops this critique. If, as I said above, the third chapter deliberately offers blueprints for tactical readers, it also uses the work of tactical readers to argue against one of the best-known practices of civic engagement: service learning. By creating their own political engagements on what are largely their own terms, I argue, my students don't "serve" the community (or their instructor), but—like the tactical readers of the first two chapters—work with greater agency. They activate language, connect across difference, and shape ideas and practices beyond a "civic" paradigm.

The final chapter extends this argument, showing how tactical practices can insert politics into all facets of academic work. I bring together current discussions in English departments and across the field of public engagement around a point of shared concern: politics. In my home discipline, large political claims are not uncommon; but they are usually grounded in little more than close textual attention. Scholars of public engagement, on the other hand, have recently begun to lament the lack of politics in their work—despite the prevalence of practices that seem, at the very least, politically inclined.

These divergent problems actually grow from a shared soil: the lack of a workable definition of politics. My final chapter, "Reconnecting the Political: Tactics, Literary Studies, and Publicly Engaged Scholarship," shows how Jürgen Habermas's theory of communicative action and deliberative democracy offers a useful definition for both literary critics and scholars of civic engagement. Habermas's theory underwrites this book, though it remains mostly in the footnotes until chapter 4. His unique ability to connect everyday conversations to systemic change can help us see the links between reading, the talk that builds bridges to wider publics, and, ultimately, impactful political action.

As this chapter recontextualizes the work of the tactical readers in light of Habermas's theory, it also makes a practical argument for faculty members about the value of tactical interventions. Improvisational, created with little support in a variety of changeable circumstances, tactical work is not only more democratic but more feasible in higher education today than large-scale public engagement projects. By understanding ourselves as tacticians, then, this final chapter suggests we might reach more diverse publics in more democratic ways, might shape more diverse political practices, and—as a result—might open up a wider range of possibilities for making necessary political change now and in the future.

Despite this closing turn toward "high theory," *Reading as Collective Action* is not a traditional scholarly book. Its most academic discussions come in the last chapter; its most technical points live in the notes. So while I aspire to speak to scholars and help change our institutions, that's not my main ambition.

In telling the stories of these tactical readers, my hope is that this work might be useful to many readers, not just those on campus. So whether you are a community organizer, a social worker, a zine editor, an activist, a scholar, or all of the above, whether you are reading this book on a college campus or at a public library or as you slump in bed with your eyes barely open in those last few minutes before sleep, I hope you will find *Reading as Collective Action* an adaptable, actionable set of blueprints. I hope it helps you use books to change our world.

1

Dissent after September 11

how poetry reclaims human rights

Within two weeks of the September 11 attacks, journalists were fired for criticizing the president, college professors were disciplined for speaking about potential motivations for terrorism, and advertisers pulled support from TV programs voicing "unpatriotic" sentiments.[1] Americans of diverse origins—particularly those with brown skin—experienced even more virulent attacks. From their ostensible compatriots, they faced increasing hostility, physical violence, and murder; governments, both national and local, resorted to explicit racial profiling and extra-legal detentions.[2] By early October, the Bush Administration had launched a war in Afghanistan and was hinting at further battles to come, pressing a narrative—borrowed from Samuel Huntington—of a "clash of civilizations." Since, as the President put it, "you are with us or with the terrorists," it was only logical that borders must be locked down and immigrants (or anyone who fit racist stereotypes of what an immigrant might look like) scrutinized.[3]

While all this was happening, poetry was circulating with unusual alacrity. "Poems flew through cyberspace across the country in e-mails from friend to friend" and from fax machine to fax machine; they echoed in museums, churches, YMCAs, and public libraries.[4] "Walking around [New York City] you would see them—stuck on light posts and phone stalls, plastered on the shelters at bus stops and the walls of subway stations" even "scrawled . . . in the ash that covered everything."[5] Poetry was a central part of "improvised memorials" on the sidewalks of many cities; "on the brick walls of police stations and firehouses, behind the mountains of flowers and between photos of the dead, poetry dominated."[6] Newspapers that hadn't published poetry for years suddenly found themselves printing verse again. "On the radio and TV, pundits have routinely taken to dusting off half-remembered verses from their school years."[7] Poetry was, the media kept repeating, "everywhere."[8]

Poetry might seem an inadequate response to the political situation I just described. But this chapter chronicles the way readers used texts as tactics to speak back to the intertwined spike in racial profiling and the rise of imperialist attitudes in the United States in the months after September 11. Taken together, the poems (re)published "everywhere" demanded recognition and provided political representation; they served simultaneously to critique the government's actions and to reclaim the rights those actions were calculated to deny.

To develop this argument, this chapter's first section offers a sort of discursive table of contents of this unbound anthology.[9] I include traditional literary critical details—what the poems said, who wrote them—and, perhaps more importantly, where they were (re)published, from city streets to tightly controlled mass media. Cataloguing the poems in this way allows me to discuss some of the thematic resonances that bind this anthology together, particularly its commitment to an inclusive, humanist unity.

In the chapter's second section, I focus on how this theme is developed and complicated, particularly by three highly circulated poems: "After the Funeral of Assam Hamady" (1971) by Sam Hamod, "Palestine" (2001) by Lorna Dee Cervantes, and Amiri Baraka's "Somebody Blew Up America" (2001). Like the rest of the anthology, these poems argue, in philosophical terms, for "recognition": the acknowledgment of the rights of "minority" communities (in this case, mostly black and brown people) to be different without sacrificing their legal equality.[10]

Not, I admit, a very shocking claim. Even people who don't pay much attention to literature often credit it with this type of work.[11] Literature is good at expressing experiences, making them intelligible—through narrative, through voice—to others. And recognition is good, as far as it goes; but I, like Nancy Fraser and many others, believe that justice today requires more than recognition, particularly when the situation is as dire as that which I describe in the first paragraph of this chapter. In addition to recognition, justice today requires political representation and, quite often, material redistribution.[12]

Thus, in the chapter's third section, I show how tactical readers not only made recognition claims but, by republishing these poems, achieved a more complex, impactful form of justice: they found ways to represent themselves where representation was otherwise unavailable. Via the republication of poems, particularly in mass media, tactical readers don't just ask to be recognized; they reclaim rights to speech, to full participation in the polity. In the months after September 11, poems were "everywhere" because readers were using texts as tactics. They brought poems into conversation with mass publics and—in a repressive and dangerous moment—both represented those who faced discrimination and worked for the redistribution of civil rights for all.

The Anthology

Much has been written about the mass circulation of W. H. Auden's lyric "September 1, 1939" (1939) in the wake of September 11. It appeared in at least thirty newspapers, all over the web, and even on "the back page of a newsletter from Minneapolis's leading food co-op."[13] It was, no doubt, the most circulated poem in the months after September 11. And, for reasons I'll discuss below, that makes sense. But as I discovered more and more references to Auden's poem and September 11, I began to wonder what other poems were out there and how they might be conversing with (or contesting) Auden. So I picked my way through the archives of national and regional newspapers, through academic books and the open web, even through the September 11 Photo Project archive at the New York Public Library, looking for other examples of poetry circulating in the months after September 11. I found a lot.

Days after the attack, Lorna Dee Cervantes's poem "Palestine" mingled with Adrienne Rich's "In Those Years" (1991) and Allen Ginsberg's "Kaddish" (1961), as well as verse by W. B. Yeats, William Blake, Carl Sandburg, and Edith Sitwell on About.com's selection "After the Attack:

Poems Worth Remembering." Two days after the attacks, bits of Emily Dickinson ("After great pain, a formal feeling comes—," 1862) and Alfred Lord Tennyson ("In Memoriam," 1850) appeared in the *New York Times.*

In mid-September, former poet laureate Robert Pinsky read Marianne Moore's philosophical poem "What Are Years?" (1941) on PBS's *NewsHour with Jim Lehrer*—just a few days before he republished it in an article with three other poems in *Slate*. Moore's poem circulated on the web, too, showing up in a selection edited by Alicia Ostriker on the site Mobylives.com, under the title "Poems for the Time," with Muriel Rukeyser, Stephen Dunn's "To a Terrorist" (1989), and others.

In October, Shakespeare's Sonnet 64 ("When I have seen by Time's fell hand defaced," 1609) showed up in the *Times* with parts of Seamus Heaney's translation of *Philoctetes* (1991), Edwin Arlington Robinson, and Shelley's "Ozymandias" (1818). The same article included a photograph of part of a poem from Constance Lindsay Skinner's *Songs of the Coast Dwellers* (1930)—a faux-indigenous book of poems—that had been posted in New York's Union Square Park.[14] Two weeks later Sonnet 64 showed up again in the Montreal *Gazette*; a few days after that, it was broadcast to radio listeners around the country on Garrison Keillor's "The Writer's Almanac." Keillor had also broadcast poems like Robert Herrick's famous ballad "To the Virgins" (1648) and a series of posthumous Charles Bukowski poems with their mordant commentary on everyday indignities.

Actors read verse by Dylan Thomas, Walt Whitman (his "Mannahatta" [1860]), Langston Hughes, "and others" every day from September 21 to October 7 in the American Wing of the Metropolitan Museum of Art.[15] Within a week of the attacks NPR anchor Scott Simon was also reading poems: Auden, but also Thomas, Whitman, and E. E. Cummings's "i go to this window" (1926). Later in September, Simon hosted Sam Hamod, who read his poem "After the Funeral of Assam Hamady." On Sunday September 16, Stephen Dunn read to an audience of more than one hundred people at the public library in Katonah, New York; and later in the month communities gathered in sixty-four libraries across Maine—a state with just over a million people—to hear Auden's poem and others as well.[16]

And of course there was Amiri Baraka. "Somebody Blew Up America" —self-published in early October as a small-circulation chapbook, a page on Baraka's website, and a staple in his public readings—zipped around the internet and the globe, eventually finding itself in the *New York Times*, the *Washington Post*, the *Wall Street Journal*, and on CNN's *Connie Chung* and Fox's *The O'Reilly Factor*.[17]

These paragraphs are something like an annotated table of contents for the anthology—unified temporally (appearing in the months after September 11), as well as, like many anthologies, by shared thematic concerns. If you'd rather, you can think of this as a minicanon with deep ties to the cultural prestige of *the* canon (hence the inclusion of Shakespeare, Dickinson, Auden, Tennyson, and other well-known anglophone poets). At various stages of considering these poems, I've used the language of the canon to talk about it.[18] But I've come to like "anthology" better for two reasons.

The word "canon" evokes, of course, the religious texts deemed acceptable by clergy; and even in its contemporary literary sense, the canon is maintained mostly through powerful institutions: "education, patronage, and journalism."[19] While some examples from this anthology are reproduced in such privileged contexts—readings of poems at colleges and museums—most appear in less-mediated spaces: websites that mix the work of award-winning poets like Adrienne Rich with unknown poets or newspapers (in the early twenty-first century, hardly the most literary of media). And, of course, many more poets get to read their poems at colleges or museums today than are accepted into the elite preserves of the canon proper. So the anthology was constructed not by scholarly norms—it eschews traditional literary-historical categories of nation or period, for instance—but by readers "lacking the specific competence" associated with canon formation and instead applying "perceptual schemes of their own ethos."[20]

The second reason I prefer anthology has to do with materiality. The canon is often abstract: an "imaginary list" as John Guillory famously put it.[21] But this anthology is material.[22] And materiality is important for understanding how these texts work in the world: a poem in a newspaper reads differently than one in an anthology of other poems; a poet's voice coming out of the radio differs from the written text. This is equally true of poems in e-mails and on websites, poems in chapbooks.

What I'm pursuing here is more than a list of poem titles, more than a table of contents in a Norton anthology. This chapter is describing the warp and weft of an anthology made of particular publications, which drew selectively on the power of "the canon" to amplify its own claims. And its varied material incarnations, as I'll show, had very real consequences, especially for the redistributive claims its creators were making. But—and this is why the idea of "anthology" might seem odd—these poems are not materially bound into a book as most anthologies are. So what, if not thread and glue, binds them together? Not style (like the famous anthology of Language Poets *In the American Tree* [1986]) or race (like *The New Black Poetry* [1969]) or generation (Donald Hall's *New Poets of England and America* [1962]). This anthology is bound first by when and where its poems were published and consumed (in the United States, in the months following September 11); but second—and more importantly—it coheres around themes and ideas.

Some themes one might expect. There is mourning:

This is the Hour of Lead—
Remembered, if outlived,
As Freezing persons, recollect the snow.[23]

There is *carpe diem*: "Gather ye rosebuds while ye may," intoned Garrison Keillor, reading Herrick's "To the Virgins" (1648) on his "Writer's Almanac" (broadcast nationally via NPR on Sunday, September 23).[24] Other poets, too, sought for tangible, sensual reality. Adam Zagajewski's "Try to Praise the Mutilated World" (2001), printed, starkly, on its own page in the *New Yorker* of September 24, invests small details—"wild strawberries, drops of wine, the dew"—with profound significance.[25]

But affirmation and joy—even if, as above, tempered with the realization that life is finite—are hardly the norm. These poems are rarely gauzy or sentimental. A surprising number, in fact, offer brutal echoes of September 11: the "blind skyscrapers" which "proclaim / The strength of Collective Man" as well as "The unmentionable odor of death" that

"Offends the September night," are familiar lines in Auden's poem. So while that poem famously ends with affirmation ("We must love one another or die"), its most brutal evocations are more consonant with other themes in the anthology.[26]

To put it another way, the majority of the poems side with the later Auden, who would disavow the power of love;[27] they echo with messages of doubt, fragmentation, and fear. Shakespeare—in a poem read on the radio and published in multiple newspapers—describes various instances of "ruin." The first, resonating with events in real time, is falling towers: "When sometime lofty towers I see down rased."[28] Shelley's "Ozymandias" ends with the "lone and level sands" of time's indifference stretching away from a crumbling statue—its "two vast and trunkless legs of stone" also evoking the Twin Towers.[29]

These repeated symbols all are marked politically as well. Shelley's "trunkless legs" are all that remain of a statue, whose "sneer of cold command" was meant to announce political might. Auden's poem touches on the perils of imperialism ranging from Thucydides's transcription of Pericles's funeral oration (a speech that praises Athenian democracy and imperialism) to "Imperialism's face / And the international wrong."[30] Shakespeare, who also draws on the metaphor of the unending battle between land and sea, links these metaphors to a political one: "interchange of state, / Or state itself confounded to decay."[31]

Jostling against these poems, so resonant in their metaphors, are philosophical questions about guilt and innocence. "What is our innocence, / what is our guilt?" opens Marianne Moore's poem, which goes on to announce: "All are / naked, none is safe."[32] Amichai—his poem published in an online anthology—describes a world of violence caused not by humans, but by their faith: "God has pity on kindergarten children" but "on grownups he has no pity at all."[33] Worse than a god's indifference, Adrienne Rich, in the last poem in About.com's anthology (again, under the heading "Poems after the Attack: Old Poems Worth Remembering"), sees violent swoops by "the great dark birds of history" as punishment for the selfishness she identifies in contemporary western culture, where "we lost track / of the meaning of *we*, of *you*."[34]

This anthology, then, eschews simple comfort. It does not turn away from the attacks but focuses, in surprisingly brutal detail, on human suffering, linking collapsing towers to collapsing states, political hubris to personal suffering. This focus is evident in notes about the conversations people had *about* the poems as well. In Maine, readers "shared their own childhood memories . . . and they called for social activism, whether to reduce the use of fossil fuels or to be more compassionate abroad."[35] At a Florida poetry reading, "Calls echoed for bloodletting. Calls echoed for peacemaking. One author wondered: Why now do we raise the flag when it remained idle at the sight of so many other spasms of injustice? Competing views were reviewed but never reviled."[36] In New York, antiwar protesters read their verses in the streets.[37]

If comfort is to be found in many of these poems, it is in ideas that echo the spaces where these poems were read and discussed. Rukeyser, writing "in the first century of world wars" suggests this suffering can create connection:

> We would try by any means
> To reach the limits of ourselves, to reach beyond ourselves,
> To let go the means, to wake.[38]

This humanist unity is persistent: "*We* must love one another or die"; "*We* would try . . . to reach beyond ourselves"; "What is *our* guilt?"[39] It would be easy to dismiss such gestures as little more than words on the page (or, even accepting their value as such, dismiss them as bland claims, too vague to do much), particularly in light of the vicious and divisive realities of this moment. Yet it's precisely because of these realities—the racial profiling, the hatred, the nationalist violence and fear—that I think these unifying ambitions merit attention. To assert a strain of humanist pluralism, however bland, was, in the face of Bush-administration xenophobia, an act of contestation.

Even discussed at this general level, it seems clear that these poems work against the incipient language of the Bush administration. Recall President Bush's late September speech declaring, "Either you are with us, or you are with the terrorists."[40] For Bush, "us" is limited, purely national; in these poems, the first-person plural maintains an inclusiveness that is far less finite and far, far less aggressive. In short, the first-person plural assertion of these poems speaks of the perils of jingoistic nationalism and the value of pluralism.

The anthology emphasizes inclusivity not only because it is composed of poems that rely on the first-person plural and make direct claims of unity, but taken together, as an anthology, these poems offer a definition of inclusion. They do so both in terms of selection and in terms of the canon. The anthology brings together views from different countries, races, classes, and genders—not to mention views ranging over two thousand years of history and representing many points on the political spectrum.[41] Even at the level of metaphor there is a grasp for inclusion; as abstract diction like "great dark birds of history" or "reach beyond ourselves" indicates, these poems are chosen, at least in part, because they are broadly applicable and might foment connections between a diversity of people.

This ideal of inclusion is also visible at a formal literary-critical level. The poems are composed in formally diverse ways: sonnets and free verse, rhyming and unrhyming. They also draw from various periods, various national literary traditions, as well as transnational traditions, since the number of translations and cases of deliberate intertextuality is noteworthy. In many respects—which would be apparent to many different audiences—tactical readers created an inclusive anthology.

Still, in an era when a bland multicultural recognition (viz. the Bush administration's own pride in its racial diversity) was the order of the day, one might rightly read general announcements of a collective "we" as, on their own, simply reaffirming a neoliberal status quo. Indeed, it would be embarrassing to confuse the assertion of an imaginary unity, one that plasters over differences and presumes we can all simply get along, with a meaningful challenge to the overt acts of discrimination, exclusion, and outright violence I describe above. But the anthology's relationship to diversity is complex. I now want to turn to the ways in which it complicates any overly simple versions of "unity" by insisting on recognition of difference. Poems by Lorna Dee Cervantes, Sam Hamod, and Amiri Baraka voice experiences of exclusion, both historical and immediate; they contest simple notions of a unified "we." In doing so, they make a powerful, affirmative claim for recognition.

Recognition

"After the Funeral of Assam Hamady" by Sam Hamod is a longish poem narrated from the perspective of a young Muslim. He, his grandfather, father, and father's friend are driving across South Dakota ("the 1950 Lincoln / ninety miles an hour") after presiding at the titular funeral.[42] As the sun begins to set, the speaker's grandfather insists the car must be stopped for *salat*. The old men climb out of the car by the roadside, but the speaker remains

> behind the wheel
> watching, my motor still running
>
> car lights scream by

Shortly after this, he announces, "I'm embarrassed to be with them."[43] So embarrassed, in fact, that while he gets out of the car at his father's insistence, he will not pray, only "stand guard."[44]

The long prayer that follows makes up nearly half the poem. It ends ("Ameen . . .") and, following a pause—it's a large white space in the original publication—the speaker, now removed from the memorial past, speaks in the present tense ("I hear them still singing") and announces he is

> trying so hard to join them
> on that old prayer blanket—
> as if the pain behind my eyes
> could be absolution[45]

In his youth, the speaker remembers feeling trapped: both Muslim and not-Muslim. Now he is doubly trapped: ashamed by his repudiation of the faith that can give him the absolution he desires. The poem expresses in these ways the difficulty of living between cultures.

Hamod's poem was not written about September 11; it was originally published as a beautiful chapbook by a small press in Wisconsin in

1971.[46] Yet in the fall of 2001, this thirty-year-old poem takes on a new and specific meaning as Hamod reads it, as I noted above, on National Public Radio. In its most obvious sense, it brings forth the voice of Muslim Americans, asserting, both in its content and by virtue of its republication, that Muslims are a threatened (hence the old woman who, driving past, "strains a gawk"[47] and the need to "stand guard") part of the social reality of the United States.

But it does more than simply assert a right to belong; it asserts a right to difference. Much of the poem is made up of the speaker's transcription and translation of the Arabic of the three older speakers: "Hysht Iyat? (What're you yelling about?)."[48] Just as the speaker expresses his position between cultures, he serves as a translator: a native informant, but one who never suppresses his own betweenness (in his tone, in his metaphors), making the reader constantly aware that he is not present solely for our understanding. Indeed, the poem's central theme is the conflictedness of its speaker's position. So while he describes the prayer in detail—"they rub their hands / then their faces / . . . their feet bare"—he does not translate the *adhan* that the three men pray, despite the fact that the words of the prayer make up nearly half the poem.[49]

Imagine someone in the fall of 2001, in Omaha or Albuquerque, flipping on the kitchen radio or starting the car to hear Hamod's voice, mid-poem, mid-prayer. Its presence—the voice, the words, the story it tells—in these private spaces is remarkable. And its message is complex. While the poem's publication in this mass media space validates the presence of Muslims as part of the social reality of the United States, it does not insist that they can be fully assimilated, or even fully understood. Even in a multicultural society, some things, the poem argues, are not available for translation.

To me, the poem makes sense as something to read after September 11. But how did it spiral out of special collections libraries (the only place besides NPR that I could get a copy) and memories of a long-ago poetry scene? Certainly not because Sam Hamod is a well-known poet. His work was published entirely by small presses, mostly in the 1960s and 1970s. His main visibility after September 11 was not as a literary figure but as a critic of the Bush administration; he published editorials in Southern California newspapers, including the *Los Angeles Times*,[50] he was a presenter on shows on BET and other channels, he lectured on college campuses about "media terrorism" and the connections between the attacks and American foreign policy.[51] While Hamod's critical role might not have been fully evident to those who encountered the poem's republication on National Public Radio, it seems likely that it was this role that made him visible to the editors at NPR who ultimately retrieved this poem from the archives in late September 2001.

Hamod's appearance on the radio—on a Saturday episode of NPR's "Weekend Edition"—presents a critical position. The poem's content explicitly gives voice to the feelings of threat experienced by Muslims in America. Presented at this moment, the poem implicitly speaks back to the crescendoing media discourse equating Islam with terrorism and, importantly, does so in the poet's voice, framed by his introduction as "president of the American Islamic Institute in San Diego, former director of the American Islamic Center of Washington, DC."[52] Hamod's poem is identified explicitly with Muslim-American reality, with the voice of a Muslim American, and is broadcast across the United States.

"After the Funeral of Assam Hamady" asserts one aspect of multicultural experience. In this anthology it represents cultural "others." In expressing his difficult position, the speaker might go one step further and help a broader public (at least partially) understand and empathize with this experience. The two poems I will now turn to express similar experiences. Yet these poems develop more forceful claims about the causes of such othering and its consequences.

An acclaimed poet, one with awards and prestigious teaching positions on her CV, Lorna Dee Cervantes doesn't usually publish her poems on websites like About.com. But a few days after September 11, she published "Palestine," dated 12 September 2001, there—a choice that seems deliberately calculated to bring her work to a wider audience than even celebrated poets typically achieve.[53]

The poem begins with two italicized lines of framing that are confessional and open but are also somewhat pedagogical, as if Cervantes is thinking of her mass audience even at the moment of composition:

Looking for some comfort in a poem. This is to PLO poet, Mahmoud Darwish:

"We travel like other people, but we return to nowhere . . . / . . . / We have a country of words. Speak. Speak so we may know the end of this travel."

(from We Travel like Other People, *the lines quoted are from his poem "Psalm 2")*

Cervantes's choice of title and this explicit note to the reader emphasize the poem's substantial intertextuality with the work of Palestinian poet and Palestine Liberation Organization activist Mahmoud Darwish. She also links—not just alludes but hyperlinks his name—to a free online collection of his work. These explicit ties to Darwish, the poem's self-dated publication, and its placement in an online anthology of poems relating to September 11 argue for an implicit connection between the attacks and US foreign policy.

This deliberate framing is interesting in itself: poets are often reluctant to offer such guides for interpretation. But it's particularly important as "Palestine" is a very difficult poem. It begins with themes of travel and exile drawn from Darwish's "We Travel like Other People" (1986); and the description of airports offers another link to the attacks, as does the mention of "a busted window / a hundred flights up." But there is no comforting "we" here—just a barrage of unanswerable questions: "Who owns / this property?" and "Who owns the key / to Heaven's Gate? Did it open?" Though the poem announces itself as "Looking for some comfort," the first stanza is brutal.

The poem's second stanza seems to ratchet down, but quickly becomes even more pointed. The speaker announces everyday tasks: opening a newspaper, a computer, a bank account. But "account" repeats and its meaning shifts from the bank account to a reckoning "for all / the terror in the world." Indeed, the speaker herself is being made to account for it, she says, as she draws attention "in crossing / the street with my child this morning, / our Indian heads and Palestinian shrouds." This is a clear description of the racial interpellation so prominent after the attacks—and its absurdity. For being Chicana, she is made to "account" for her presence. "With what do we pay?" she asks, bending the accounting metaphor back to the economic, and smacking the reader with yet another unanswerable question.

While Cervantes would be well within her rights to reject out of hand the expectation that she "account" for September 11, the poem's third stanza does offer a kind of accounting. She looks back to Darwish's work, paraphrasing another of his poems with her question: "what / if the source of death / is not the dagger / or the lie?"[54] Her answer to this question might be understood as her accounting. The "source of death" is

> Buried deep
> in the human rubble.
> Closer to God
> than thee.

This inverted allusion to the Christian hymn "Nearer, My God, to Thee" suggests historical religious conflict—the legacy of the Crusades, for instance—explicitly linking Christianity with causation (the cause is "Closer to God," as the enjambment would have it) amidst the "rubble" of September 11.

I've spent a long time (far longer, I suspect, than the average About.com reader would) puzzling over the poem. Those impossible questions, the brutal enjambments, the shifting senses of words like "accounting." It really is a difficult poem. So what stands out? Like Hamod, Cervantes expresses the difficulty of being caught between cultures.[55] And like Hamod she translates racial profiling for a diverse audience—a new insight, it's safe to say, for many readers of About.com. This is, to me, the key graspable moment in the poem. But Cervantes goes further than Hamod, framing her own experience with geopolitical analysis. From its announced and hyperlinked intertextuality with a "PLO poet," Cervantes's poem pushes a reader to comprehend a link between Islam, evangelical Christianity, and the United States' support for Israel—or perhaps more pertinently between the attacks of September 11 and the ongoing struggle between Israel and Palestine.[56]

Even if the About.com reader didn't "get" Cervantes's poem, it's hard to miss these implications. And they are just the sort of thing that got many prominent figures in trouble in the months after the attacks. That Cervantes broaches this conversation in a poem, published just days after September 11, certainly merits some attention.

If Cervantes opened a risky conversation, Amiri Baraka amplified it. His "Somebody Blew Up America"—no doubt one of the most-discussed poems published about September 11—takes up these linkages even more adamantly. Baraka self-published the poem on his website on October 1, 2001, then, later that month, in a small press print edition (published in Oakland; across the country from his home base in Newark).[57] In the following months, Baraka read the poem or had it read in "Africa; Portugal, Spain, Switzerland, Italy; on German radio by an actor" and at various colleges (schools Baraka mentions include Amherst, Iowa, Yale, and North Carolina) as well as "programs of all sorts, venues of various descriptions."[58]

It was only a year later that the poem became part of a well-known kerfuffle, pilloried for its anti-Semitism in the form of its leading questions of "Who knew the World Trade Center was gonna get bombed / Who told 4000 Israeli workers at the Twin Towers / To stay home that day."[59] It was also held up for censure for its particularly harsh shaming of major African American political figures like "Tom Ass Clarence" or Colin Powell, rechristened "Colon," from whose mouth "doo doo" comes. After much media tumult, Baraka was condemned by the Anti-Defamation League (a longstanding antagonist) and, ultimately, New Jersey's Government, at whose pleasure he was then serving as Poet Laureate.[60]

Whatever the poem presumes in the way of conspiracy theories, it seems to question its own terms by insisting, again and again, that the reader question whatever story she is told about September 11. Prefaced with what "They say" about a "barbaric / A Rab, in / Afghanistan" plotting and planning, Baraka asks how we can trust what "they" say, since "they" are the ones

That have murdered black people
Terrorized reason and sanity
Most of humanity, as they pleases

Indeed, nearly two-thirds of the lines in the poem begin with "who":

(who say?)
Who do the saying
Who is them paying
Who tell the lies
Who in disguise
. . . .
Who/ Who / Who/
Who stole Puerto Rico
Who stole the Indies, the Philippines, Manhattan[61]

Imagine this poem read in Baraka's highly performative register. The interrogation is intense, whether the audience imagines itself sharing in the questions—or being interrogated. And how differently would audiences in Africa or Germany hear these words than in the United States? Consider this poem flying at its audience in an e-mail (I'll cite such an example below). Do the questions seem pointed? Simply rhetorical? Do they evoke Moore's "What is our innocence / what is our guilt?" Or are they, like those in Cervantes's poem, unanswerable?

The text's anaphoric inquiry comes to a climax in its final moments, when it attempts to forge a partnership between its speaker and its reader in the investigation of these crimes:

We hear the questions rise
In terrible flame like the whistle of a crazy dog

Like the acid vomit of the fire of Hell
Who and Who and WHO (+) who who
Whoooo and whooooooOOOOOOooooOoooo![62]

The reader is invited to become a questioner, unified (again) in the first-person plural "we." The poem wants them to join the speaker in trying to figure out not who committed these atrocities, but who—on some deeper level—caused them.

Perhaps "Somebody Blew Up America" is less directly concerned than "Palestine" or "After the Funeral of Assam Hamady" with expressing an othered position. There is no "I" here, no confessional self. Yet the poem—particularly in its mass-mediated incarnation—was repeatedly and explicitly tied to Baraka's race; and it is worth noting that the poem begins with "the Klan" and "the Skin heads" and holds up African American political figures for particular censure. Even considering its global ambitions, "Somebody Blew Up America" is, like the other poems I have been discussing, an expression of a particular othered American experience. Yet its challenge to its readers goes far beyond simply asking for recognition. It does not ask just to be seen and included but uses the attacks as a launching point to reinvestigate historical misdeeds from colonization to slavery to Rudy Giuliani's neoconservative policies.

As part of this anthology, Baraka, Cervantes, and Hamod add their voices to the humanist unity I traced in this chapter's first section: they are united by (most obviously) their shared genre but also by linguistic commonalities (questions, for example) and overlapping concerns (the integration of geopolitics into verse). But they also offer critical reflection on the limitations and perils built into such unity. They use different voices, different rhetorical strategies; and they give voice to different experiences—those, for instance, who might suffer cultural and physical violence as Muslims (or, as in Cervantes's poem, those who might be racially profiled as Muslims). In challenging their reader to understand those experiences as part of a broader set of questions about American culture and law, about global history and oppression, the anthology presents a focused critique of imperialism and jingoistic nationalism, voiced by W. H. Auden, William Shakespeare, and Marianne Moore, as well as by Sam Hamod, Lorna Dee Cervantes, and Amiri Baraka.

Read as such, the anthology operates, as literature is often understood to do, within the paradigm of political recognition. It seeks not just acknowledgment of human commonality but respect for distinct "cultural value" and "equal *opportunity* for achieving social esteem."[63] It argues that contemporary democracy requires far more than simply praising "diversity" and acknowledging difference in the cultural realm while maintaining a discriminatory (quasi-legal) status quo.

And poems are a particularly good medium for such an argument. As Iris Marion Young—a philosopher, not a literary critic—has pointed out, poems, whether grounded in the lyric tradition (Hamod, Cervantes) or in Baraka's more radical, discursive approach, use strategies that enrich communication from emotional appeals to symbols and figures of speech. Democratic inclusion, Young writes, "requires an expanded conception of political communication, both in order to identify modes of internal inclusion and to provide an account of more inclusive possibilities of attending to one another in order to reach understanding." [64]

Using this array of rhetorical techniques, the anthology very effectively represents not only the experiences and sensibilities of a diverse group of people but does so in a surprisingly diverse number of ways. In this, it makes what I'd call a strong recognition claim. Yet in the months after September 11, claims for recognition may have been insufficient. It was, as I've been repeating, a time when people with brown skin—and anyone who dissented—might experience attacks both physical and rhetorical. People were harassed for walking across the street. The president was calling for a clash of civilizations. It was not a good time for dissent.

This was particularly true in mass media. After September 11, the media (as one scholarly analysis puts it) "follow[ed the] lead of [the] Bush administration."[65] In this climate, those who would offer critique could say what they wanted to say but only if no one could hear it. To paraphrase Marx, they could not represent themselves; they must be represented. Poems, in this moment, provided an important tool for such representation. If these poems had appeared only in marginal venues, if they had been read, I mean, by only the people who normally read such poems, their political significance would've been less remarkable. In the following section, I turn to how the tactical readers who circulated these poems, particularly in public spaces and mass media, presented something more than just another literary claim for recognition.

Representation and Justice

Literary studies is a field based on studying representation—the representation of the world in words. And when scholars make political claims about literature, they often like to imply that "subversive currents of social agitation will flow, as if by fiat, from their favorite piece of performance art."[66] But the space between representation within the text or within the literary canon and broad social recognition is vast; if a poem falls in a small circulation journal, does anyone hear it? How much recognition—to say nothing of other facets of justice like political representation or redistribution—does a poem produce if only a few people read it?

To put this in more philosophical terms—borrowed from Nancy Fraser—poems that make recognition claims often do so outside of a "stable framework in which claims can be equitably vetted" and without "institutionalized agencies and means of redress."[67] Literature, by virtue of being written, hardly guarantees recognition or representation (to, again, say nothing of economic redistribution). My point is simple: scholars (of literature, of public engagement) need to confirm that the radical ideas they study are really shaping cultural recognition, political representation, and/or redistributive change before making grand political claims of the sort I make here.

After September 11, I've just argued, poems were part of actuating recognition. But perhaps even more necessary was representation—the act of creating a sense of "social belonging" as well as enabling participation in "the procedures that structure public processes of contestation."[68] The state failed (and not just passively) to guarantee the rights to life and liberty of many people: the right to walk down the street, the right to be a Muslim (or to look like someone's idea of a Muslim), the right to disagree with the President. While the Bill of Rights *recognized* those rights, it became necessary not just to argue for them, but to actuate them, as they were significantly curtailed.[69] Even when the law establishes something, sometimes it needs (re)claiming. Representation is a key tool for such reclamation.

This unbounded anthology was these tactical readers' means to representation. In this ugly political environment, which was in part enabled and augmented by the mass media, readers used texts as tactics to speak, to dissent, and ultimately to represent their positions in these arguments. In a remarkable example of everyday politics, poems—they were "everywhere," remember—took oppositional arguments and shared them widely, actuating free speech rights and representing these diverse, dissenting communities in a wider public discussion.

The foundation of this work seems to have been the circulation of poems in private e-mails, on listservs frequented by poets, and in small-press poetry magazines.[70] In such venues people communicate with those who share their interests. This communication begins to develop language: in this case, identifying poems that can powerfully give voice to their interests and concerns. But as the poems spiraled out of such particular and limited spaces—free speech zones that were free only because they were so marginal that those who would disapprove of their speech didn't notice them—their impact became more noticeable. They flew through other channels as more readers became part of the labor of circulation. One writer mentions someone finding a copy of "September 1, 1939" in the photocopier at a high school; a college student publishes an essay (dismayed, but engaged) about receiving Baraka's poem via an e-mail listserv of a campus peace network;[71] multiple news accounts mention people taking it upon themselves to recirculate.[72]

And, as I noted at the start, the poems zipping through e-mails and passing from hand to hand via Xerox also appeared on streets and walls, on TV, in newspapers, and on massively popular websites. There they spoke louder, reached wider audiences. This anthology, as it reaches more and more readers, supports changes that are not just personal but social and, ultimately, legal. At one level, this is just simple math. More people read About.com than read the Buffalo Poetics listserv; more people would see a poem chalked on a sidewalk, than in a zine distributed at a radical bookstore.[73] In September 2001, over a million people were subscribers to the *New York Times*; a poem published there would (do I need to say it?) have more impact than it would in most poetry magazines.[74] And sheer quantity—copies, page views—isn't the only way poems were effectual. In these mass venues, poems worked differently than they might in more familiar habitats. Their public speech, perhaps most notably, was made visible by contrast. Assonant or alliterative, metaphoric or similetic, anaphoric or chiasmic, rhythmic or free, poems are different. On the streets—recited, photocopied—they offered stark contrast from the blaring, high-gloss ads of contemporary capitalism. That poem chalked on the sidewalk transformed a fairly invisible space into a discursive place.[75]

In mass media, this contrast is only enhanced. In nightly newscasts or on the radio, poems' rhythmic and tonal qualities contrasted with the standard diction of anchors. In print, they were typographically distinct: bordered by far wider margins than the typical feature on the pages of newspapers; published in sidebars, in italicized block quotes leaping out—even to skimmers—from the text of their articles. On the web, too, their ragged justification (and white space) stands out. Poetry, as it flows through these various mass media sources, stands out aurally, visually. In these contexts we don't need genre theory to recognize its difference. And not only do poems stand out linguistically, but they also carry with them a complicated prestige. Poets are no longer celebrities in the way Whitman or T. S. Eliot were, but Romantic conceptions of the artist—the visionary, the outsider—persist, and poetry still offers something discursive language cannot. Poetry, despite all the laments about its death, is still, somehow, special. A columnist in the *Atlanta Journal-Constitution*, writing on September 23 about the massive resurgence of art, claimed that poets with "their heads in the clouds, far removed from important daily concerns" have a "heightened perception of the world [that] is an invaluable source of reality."[76] So if part of the anthology's power was derived from how the literary features expressed their difference from the more mundane language that surrounded them, another part was derived from its status as literary. These aspects are clearly mutually reinforcing.

In themselves, the positive contrasts (newswriting versus poetry) seem almost too obvious to note. But the contrast—particularly in the mass media—is not purely textual. This was a moment, remember, in which television anchor Dan Rather could declare, "George Bush is the President, he makes the decisions, and you know, as just one American, he wants me to line up, just tell me where"; in which faulty reporting—most famously about links between Al Qaeda and Saddam Hussein's regime—aided the spread of the American war into Iraq. As Judith Butler put it, "reporting itself has become a speech act in the service of the military operations."[77] Circulating in the mass media flows that were greasing the wheels of war, these poems stood out not just textually, but in the ideas they offered.

Indeed, as the poems appeared in mass media, their contrast—and their power—was even acknowledged fairly directly by those recirculators. The *New York Times* introduced the block of poems it published in early October with this rather unjournalistic language: "Here," wrote the editors, "are some selections from poems that have been circulating among people in the past few weeks."[78] The vague nouns "some selections," "people," "few weeks," and the passive-voice construction betray the *Times*'s uncertainty about printing these poems at all. Why, one can almost hear the editors asking, are we printing a bunch of poems? The answer draws its justification from those "people" who have been "circulating" the poems "in the past few weeks." Put another way, the *Minneapolis Star Tribune*, publishing "September 1, 1939," explained directly that the poem "has been widely distributed on the Internet in the last month as readers have noted its relevance to the events of Sept. 11."[79] The Montreal newspaper the *Gazette* (quoting Shakespeare, Auden, Robinson Jeffers, and others), noted that "poems are being read publicly, are being posted at memorial sites; poems are circulating by e-mail in an unprecedented way."[80] Mass media publication drew its legitimacy from public circulation.

In other examples, newspapers justified their republication with their own kinds of proof: pictures of people copying poems onto sidewalks,[81] explicit solicitation of poems from their readers (while noting they do "not print poetry in the letters to the editor section at any time. However . . ."),[82] think pieces—quoting local poets and academics—about what poetry means and does.[83] They also cited the publication of poems in other media; one newspaper, in the lede of a story accompanying its own publication of poems, writes, "It's no accident we've been hearing more [poetry] on National Public Radio."[84] While affirming the complicated prestige that poetry maintains, these evocations all speak to an element of uncertainty not only in the reporting about the explosion of poetry but in understanding how and why newspapers themselves are part of that explosion. They feel compelled, but they don't know where exactly the explosion comes from.

The propulsion, of course, is the work of everyday politics, the actions of the poetry circulators drawing on poetry to reclaim rights denied. And while the mass media dither a bit about what all this means, here the important point is not how the mass media frame the poems but the fact that mass media are circulating these ideas at all. Mass media don't know why poetry is everywhere, but the media are still helping to put poetry *everywhere*.[85]

So yes, as many critics have pointed out, the "public sphere" in the twenty-first century is, if it exists at all, rarely a space for "critical publicity." And yes, it not only fails to represent the beliefs of various cultural blocs but presents, in fact, the ideas of massive media conglomerates—with myriad ties to the political establishment—as being "our" feelings or thoughts.[86] And yes, concerns about co-optation, that mass media are "the prime institutional site for the construction of the consent that defines the new, hegemonic mode of domination," are legitimate.[87] Yet these poems clearly signify that the mass mediated public sphere remains a contested space. The poems dissent from other, more dominant, narratives. And there's little evidence of co-optation: the anthology was built from the ground up, by readers using texts as tactics; in the media, poems were mostly treated with respect.[88]

But perhaps more importantly, to spend too long on such critiques ignores the larger benefits of this circulation. As mass media bring poems out of literary spaces and to the attention of passers-by on the streets, casual internet surfers, and mass media elites—to masses of people aloof from both poetry and this anthology's particular politics—the contestation is broadcast widely. It reaches more of those inherently sympathetic people who are looking for conversation and confirmation; it reaches more people who aren't sure what they think; and it reaches those who would turn down a pamphlet critiquing imperialism but who stumble upon these contestatory ideas in poems, whether on the radio or TV, whether in the *Sarasota Herald-Tribune* or the *Chicago Defender* or the *New York Times*. As the poems spiral out into the world, they "accord [a more] equal voice in public deliberations and fair representation in public decision-making" to those who are marginalized;

they represent—in Fraser's sense—victims of racial profiling (and their allies) in fighting for a more just world.[89]

It may seem like an obvious thing to say, but these poems' ability to reach more and more people is the foundation of their political work. One of the essential rights infringed at this moment was the right of dissent; so to engage in massively public (poetic) speech was not just to ask for acknowledgment of oppression or rights but to actively reclaim those rights, to resist oppression. To publish poems that offer a direct critique of racial profiling, to publish poems that question the value of the state in the same mass media flows that were agitating against potential internal enemies and for imperial war was essentially political. The anthology retakes rights denied—rights of speech in general, but also particular speech for particularly raced (and racially profiled) peoples. In their blend of recognition and representation, the poems exemplify the political potential of literature. And for that justice claim to carry weight, the poems need the mass media. Any contrarian sentiment—any dissenting claim, whether for representation, recognition, or redistribution—will hardly achieve its political ambitions if it lives only in private or marginal spaces. The poems have to move through communicative action within limited lifeworlds, among limited publics, and out toward multiple publics. Poems, again, serve as bridges.[90]

The appearance of poems in mainstream media, following their appearance "everywhere" else, suggests a crack (however slight) in the repressive legal formation in the weeks and months after September 11. And this crack, I would argue, offers the basis for a new political formation—one that, contrary to the many aftereffects of September 11, encouraged pluralism and deliberation, attempted to situate cultural "others" not just as part of America (a part that might one day be marginalized by an oppressive tolerance and the next subjected to atavistic persecution) but as voices empowered to contest that culture.

So as fighter jets revved for Afghanistan, casual readers encountered lines like Baraka's raucous and echoing "who told the lies?" or Auden's "there is no such thing as the State" or Shakespeare's "state itself confounded to decay" or Rukeyser's "try to find each other, / To construct peace, to make love, to reconcile" or Cervantes's "With what do we pay."[91] As people were racially profiled, attacked, and murdered, readers stumbled upon lines like Yeats's "somewhere / A man is killed, or a house burned, / Yet no clear fact to be discerned"; or Sophocles's (in Heaney's translation), "Human beings suffer, / They torture one another, / They get hurt and get hard"; or Moore's "What is our innocence, / what is our guilt?"[92] These encounters, between literary words and wide audiences, are representational—not, I want to repeat, as a metonym, the way representation is often thought of in literary circles. The circulation of these poems isn't politics on the same order as including writers of particular racial or cultural origins within the canon. Rather, the poems become the voices of these oppressed groups—and their allies—manifested as a discursive presence; the anthology puts forth their arguments to a wide array of publics. In spaces where the critique, for instance, of racial profiling after the attacks might well have gone unheard, this anthology brings it forward.[93] It *is* political representation.

And though I evoked Marx's "Eighteenth Brumaire of Louis Bonaparte" (1852) above, it's not quite the situation Marx was describing, either. In 1848, Louis Napoleon represents the unrepresentable peasants becoming, in Marx's reading, "master[,] authority over them."[94] Here the anthology shows us representation of a different order: an instance of humans as they "make their own history" not "just as they please in circumstances they choose for themselves; rather they make it in present circumstances, given and inherited."[95] Readers used texts as tactics to speak in venues where they otherwise couldn't have said a word. And this poetic speech, I've argued, should be understood to successfully make claims not just for recognition, but for representation.

To put it another way, it's not hard to find poems that make recognition claims (or scholars quick to make those claims for poems). But in the months after September 11, 2001, tactical readers brought poems to a mass public and, in doing so, used poetry to make much more remarkable—and much more politically impactful—claims of recognition *and* representation.

Their work offers a political example worth following. It also helps illustrate the shift from thinking about texts as texts to engaging texts as tactics. Attention to *what* texts say and *how* they say it is important, but it's *where* and *to whom* they say it that makes them capable of changing things in the world. In its mass public use, literature has a role to play in everyday politics; it can, through recognition and representation, challenge dominant narratives and reclaim rights, as this chapter has shown.

But using texts as tactics can also help communities engage in another aspect of justice: acts of material redistribution that get people the things they need to survive, "the resources they need in order to interact with others as peers."[96] To make that case, I had to leave the library, the databases, and—in part—my role as an "expert." I had to go track down readers (like those who were behind the circulation of poems after September 11) in action. I had to find them working within their communities and talk to them about what they were discovering in texts. I wanted—as Julie Ellison has written of the work of Imagining America (the national consortium that advocates for the arts in public life)—to democratize "the canon literally enough to enter in the joint discovery of literary knowledge with non-academics."[97] Meeting those folks, I learned a lot more about how literature can become political than even my closest readings of Adorno had taught me. That's the story of the next chapter.

2

The Grapes of Wrath and the Great Recession

literature gets people what they need

It is the last day of February in 2009, and Jackson, like many other small towns in Michigan, is hurting. On Michigan Avenue, Jackson's main drag, parking is ample. The sun blasts off the storefronts: many are empty, some lacking even "For Lease" signs. A few people hawk antiques, candles, and trinkets for the invisible tourists. Despite the upbeat pop music piped in through hidden speakers, the street feels abandoned. It's a rare bright day in a long winter, but the future still looks bleak.

Jackson has been feeling this way for years. It's a familiar story in the upper Midwest. Midcentury, the city swelled to thirty-five thousand people and survived thanks to the unionized, blue-collar jobs that came from Detroit, seventy-five miles away. As those jobs trickled away through the 1980s and 1990s, Jackson stalled; it got poorer, grayer, quieter. Earlier in the month, Jackson's largest auto parts manufacturer started offering buyouts to its workers. In a few months, General Motors will declare bankruptcy.

While it's quiet on Michigan Avenue this Saturday, there's action across town in an elementary school gym with walls the color of a manila folder. People are setting up card tables and booths. The sodium lights hum. Someone strums chords from Woody Guthrie's "Dustbowl Refugee." A woman is hanging portraits near a giant replica soup pot cooking over a giant replica campfire. Both the pot and the fire are constructed of canned food gathered for the United Way food drive that will collect over four hundred cans during March. Nearby a table stacked with free copies of John Steinbeck's *The Grapes of Wrath* waits. The book inspired this event—and it's footing the bill.

Perhaps it is not surprising that in Jackson in early 2009 Steinbeck's 1939 novel found new popularity. Its historical relevance was clear as the worst economic downturn since the Great Depression unfolded in a series of intermeshed crises: imploding subprime mortgages, toppling financial institutions, collapsing industrial production, and massive government bailouts. The book was, according to the *Washington Post*, in "high demand" in various parts of the country.[1] But what happened that morning in February in a school gym in Jackson wasn't just promoting this simple historical correspondence. It was a complex social practice based on Steinbeck's novel: as a piece of literature, as a historical document, and as a means to everyday politics. The Jackson Services Fair was the product of tactical reading. Its organizers had read Steinbeck well; and the fair drew particularly on two crucial chapters—those chronicling the month the Joads spend in the Weedpatch Camp—to apply the novel's central philosophy for addressing poverty: collective, grassroots action supported by the government. The inspiration for this intervention would not be obvious to people who had never read the book, perhaps not even to people who had read it. Yet their reading took some of the text's imagined solutions and made them manifest.

This example of tactical reading might appear quite different from the last chapter. And it's true, the focus here is more on readers and their interactions with texts than on the work readers can ask texts to do on their behalf. But here, too, literature brings people together, catalyzing a mass public; and here, too, readers engage in acts of recognition and representation. At this point, however, I want to emphasize a third aspect of justice: material redistribution. *The Grapes of Wrath* helped these readers to understand—and connect with—people different from them; it shaped their ideas and practices about how redistribution might help those people. And they didn't keep these ideas to themselves. In what follows, I'll describe the Services Fair—and other tactical reading practices, both in Jackson and in Knoxville, Tennessee—and the inventive ways these readers linked Steinbeck's novel with redistribution in its more traditionally economic sense. The evidence and descriptions come mostly from interviews done with readers when I visited Jackson and Knoxville the summer after the events this chapter describes took place. I talked to librarians and community organizers and physicists and ministers; I talked to an elementary school principal, a grant writer and a mayor, publicists and marketers, desk clerks, students, artists, and a handful of retired folks.

Some of them wrote grants and organized programming; some solely attended the programs; nearly all discussed the book in reading groups or book clubs. To participants I asked twenty-five questions; to facilitators I asked thirty. Both covered demographic information about age, race, work, and education as well as general responses to the text (which characters they liked and disliked; what scenes they remembered most clearly; how they felt about them).[2] Along with their stories, many shared with me traces of their collective reading: promotional materials, programs for lectures, photographs.

As this chapter tells their stories, I also pursue an argument about the National Endowment for the Arts program that financed these reading practices. The Big Read advocates for community-building, mostly based in book clubs; but I'll argue that what Steinbeck's novel does in the hands of these tactical readers is both more far reaching and more politically radical than that. "Community" is a nice, but vague, political ambition. These readers use Steinbeck's novel to foment something more powerful and more connected—something that goes beyond the text and shapes the lives of thousands of people and their disparate communities.

The Services Fair

When the booths are set up, the gym of the Lincoln School opens, spilling out the smell of cafeteria food. The musician, Bill Jamerson, strums more "Dust Bowl Ballads" (inspired, of course, by John Ford's film of *Grapes*) and Depression-era blues. Patrons arrive and move through the gym, talking quietly with the people in the booths. Representatives from the Community Action Agency, a federally funded, locally operated clearinghouse for social services, are ready to talk about their programs—from helping with tax returns to Head Start schooling, neighborhood planning to microloans.[3] Big Brothers Big Sisters of America has a booth; so does Marriage Matters Jackson, a nonprofit working to maintain stable families; the Center for Family Health, a provider of medical services for underserved populations has a representative on call as well. Along with these federally funded groups, other nonprofit services set up shop for the day: disAbility Connection, a local nonprofit supporting people with disabilities; Love, INC., a religious group (INC stands for In the Name of Christ) offering immediate financial support to people who can't pay essential bills. Other booths include Catholic Charities, the Jackson County Data Network, the Girl Scouts, and (of course) the Jackson District Library.

As people move between the booths, some stop to look at the photographs hanging on the walls. These images were shot by Kate Lambert Lee, a working-class mother and nontraditional college undergraduate, who has lived her whole life in Jackson. Lee's installation, *Faces of Poverty*, showcases a number of local women. Wanda Beavers—lit from behind, pursing her lips—is determined but not humorless; in another image one of her granddaughters stares into the camera with an open face. Betty Williams, a single mother of five, has her hand pressed to her chest, looking serious, emphatically midsentence. Ashley Trusty stands, slightly bemused, in the bathroom of her apartment as her two kids brush their teeth. Text telling the women's stories of perseverance—car crashes and new friendships; families lost and recovered; the routinely impossible daily grind of single parenthood—accompanies the images.

The collection also includes an image of Kerry Hart in her comfortable living room. Her story is one of growing up in poverty. Hart's narrative contrasts with the others—she lives with her husband, Jon Hart; more on him soon—and is clearly meant to suggest possibilities. It ends with a quote that illuminates one commonality of the photographs: "It is our duty," she tells us, "to understand that the success of an individual is not generally due to their independence, but rather the support of those around them. We must find a method to support people when their own systems are not enough."[4] Indeed, each of the women acknowledges external support—from Head Start, from community groups, from adult education programs—as part of her survival.

Like much of the gym's ambience (from the music to the free lunch to the stacks of canned food) *Faces* deliberately evokes a precursor with ties to *Grapes of Wrath*: Dorothea Lange's dustbowl images, particularly that series' indelible *Migrant Mother*. In both its aesthetic allusion and in the accompanying text, Lambert Lee's work helps explain the purpose of this gathering. There were music and art, free books and free lunch; there were immediate services and advice from services agencies. And there were speeches by people with political power both in and beyond Jackson, particularly Mark Schauer, whom Jackson had recently elected to the US House of Representatives. There were even free buses to bring people from across town. The point was to connect people with people and with systems—public or private; city, state, or federal—that could support them when they needed it.

A space like this—part book fair, part block party, part art show, part temporary social services agency—is rare.[5] We are not inclined to think about libraries as part of our structure of social services, nor books (especially "classics" by Dead White Men) as aligned with the delivery of services to people living in poverty today. But not only were reading and social services joined here; the book (with help from the National Endowment for the Arts) was bankrolling the event.

The Jackson Services Fair kicked off the month-long reading program known as the Big Read, a program created—according to Dana Gioia, the poet, former General Foods CEO, and National Endowment for the Arts chair—to return reading to an "essential place in American culture."[6] The program has two aims: to "encourage reading for pleasure and enlightenment" and to "make us connect with our communities."[7] It posits a precise link between the two, often in the form of book clubs. The previous fall, the NEA had awarded Jackson a grant of $20,000 to support major events devoted specifically to the book (panel discussions, author readings, and the like); events using the book as a point of departure (film screenings, theatrical readings, and so forth); and book discussions in diverse locations and aimed at a wide range of audiences.[8]

In Jackson I certainly saw ample evidence of such practices. Jackson hosted five screenings of John Ford's *The Grapes of Wrath* (as well as *Of Mice and Men* [1939], other period films such as the Shirley Temple vehicle *Curly Top* [1935], and more contemporary features including *Cradle Will Rock* [1999]). The library hosted lectures by Rick Wartzman—whose popular history of Steinbeck's hostile reception in California, *Obscene in the Extreme* (2008), had just been published—as well as community presentations about the Depression-era Civilian Conservation Corps and Dorothea Lange's photographs. There was a week dedicated to Kit Kittredge, a popular American Girl doll, whose backstory is set in the Depression; the library hosted a display of the doll and showed the contemporary film about Kit's middle-class family. Jackson High School hosted a poetry contest (its theme was "Meeting the Challenges of Hard Times"); and musicians performed Steinbeck-themed songs. Even pastors gave sermons about *Grapes*. And, of course, there were book groups. They met in the library, in restaurants, and in homes around town. Over the course of the month, the library gave away about 1,600 copies of *Grapes of Wrath* and estimated that more than two thousand people read the book.

But the kick-off event, at least according to the Big Read's promotional literature, is the program's centerpiece: a chance to entice new readers, to set the tone for the month, and to encourage participation. At Jackson's kick-off, program organizers and politicians followed Big Read expectations, handing out free books and reader's guides. Yet the event was clearly about much more than reading. In planning, organizers had filled their calendar for the month fairly easily. But they wrestled with the kick-off—the debate continuing until just a few months before that last day of February. Some organizers argued for hosting a soup or bread line as a way to re-create a sense of living in the Depression; but Jon Hart, a community organizer with Jackson's Community Action Agency, was worried. "I thought it would just go to nostalgia. I wanted to get involved so we could paint the picture of now, rather than then. There's no harm in knowing then, [but] I don't want people to think 'Oh, it was seventy years ago, and everything's fine now.'"[9] The ultimate outcome was something, in Hart's words, "more active." The event was certainly active in the way it used the economic and social clout of the novel (and the Big Read) to produce a space for political action inflected by literary sensibilities.

Its unique nature also presented some key questions. The next morning's *Jackson Citizen Patriot* implicitly broached one in its lede: "Stephanie Eddy hadn't heard of 'The Grapes of Wrath' before this weekend, but knows she will enjoy the book."[10] The piece goes on to link Eddy—who had been out of work since her employer shut down almost a year before—with the poverty many Jackson residents were facing. But the connection appears, at least initially, somewhat forced. Despite the headline that proclaims "Big Read Book Strikes a Chord with Jackson Residents," the article focuses mostly on the Services Fair and CAA's role in the community. The only invocation of reading comes in the inverse: Eddy wasn't reading—hadn't even heard of—Steinbeck's novel.

Grapes as Blueprint

After being burned out of the Hooverville near Bakersfield, their first stop in California, the Joads arrive at the government camp with a jolt: "Tom turned in. The whole truck leaped into the air and crashed down again."[11] The jolt is a literal announcement of the camp's self-protection—the speed bump, the guard explains, protects children—but also a symbol of the shocking difference between the living conditions that have prevailed throughout the novel and what exists beyond the speed bump. The Joads "ain't been treated decent for a long time," in Tom's words. With hot water, well-ordered streets, a self-policing public, and grassroots representative democracy, the camp is, indeed, decent.[12]

The Grapes of Wrath shows, with brutal clarity, that Californians' reactions to the migrants ranged from calculated indifference to murder. The camps—according to Farm Securities Administration (FSA) plans from spring 1935—should have provided refuge to the approximately two-hundred-thousand-person reserve army of labor then wandering through the state looking for work, food, and shelter.[13] This plan proved impracticable, however, as attacks from the Associated Farmers successfully stymied attempts by "red" bureaucrats from Washington to intervene.[14] Ultimately only a handful of camps were built as part of a pilot program.

The camps that were built carried the strong impress of one man—Tom Collins, the "Tom, who lived it" in Steinbeck's dedication to the book. Collins's vision for the camps was remarkable for its coherence and generosity. The camps were not "cold, bureaucratically run" or "bristling with rules."[15] Instead, as Steinbeck wrote in his newspaper coverage of the migrants, "From the first, the intent of the management has been to restore the dignity and decency that had been kicked out of the migrants by their intolerable mode of life"—a dignity he defines as "a register of a man's responsibility to the community."[16] Though the phrase seems overwritten, the last clause is noteworthy. Steinbeck doesn't offer a vague, nice-feeling "community"; his premise involves action and mutual responsibility.

Camps operated as grassroots democracies. Each "unit" of the camp elected a "town council" as well as one representative to the "Camp Committee"—a central governing body—and multiple representatives to camp-wide committees dealing with "fire, recreation, children's playground, children's welfare, and the governing board of the Women's Club."[17] Along with producing a structure in which the migrants could self-govern for most needs, the camps also offered more material support beyond the infrastructure of bathrooms, roads, running water, and dances. Managers were tasked with teaching basic sanitation practices: how to wash hands before eating, how to clean dishes afterwards. They also directed more material sustenance. Through the women's committee, short-term financial support for families to buy groceries could be disbursed; for migrants in long-term poverty, camp managers would attempt to facilitate application to government agencies for support.[18] Such historical accounts comport closely with the details of Steinbeck's novel: the respectful solicitousness of the manager, Jim Rawley; the Joad children's confusion with flush toilets; the disbursement of emergency funds through the women's committee.

These services were—not at all coincidentally—also available at the Jackson Services Fair. In both the fictional camp and the Services Fair, people in need could find health and disability services; they could receive food in the form of a free lunch; they could find an agency, like Love INC, that could help with paying overdue bills. Agencies were primed to offer support with child welfare (Girl Scouts, Big Brothers Big Sisters of America) and guidance in basic skills, from paying taxes to maintaining healthy relationships. While the elementary school gym couldn't be turned into a shelter for the homeless, at the Services Fair they could learn about CAA's various programs to find homes for the homeless or to help freeze foreclosure proceedings. These programs, notably, appear in the narratives of Kate Lambert Lee's *Faces of Poverty*, as well. And while there was no dance (the Government Camp had the "best dances in the county" as everyone in the novel repeats), there was music.[19]

In elaborating these specific connections between the text and the fair, I mean to establish that the mode of tactical reading on display here is not purely thematic. The Services Fair's organizers did not just note a broad connection (in this case, "poverty" or "economic depression") but engaged with a specific aspect of the text: the way government-sponsored groups can help those living in poverty, not only with support, but by creating "decent" spaces for them to exist, even temporarily. So while Jackson's Services Fair clearly is not Steinbeck's Weedpatch brought to life, it draws its organizational principles from the fictional camp.

It is, then, hardly a surprise that many of the readers I interviewed mentioned the camp. Often they evoked it in response to my question about what scenes they recalled most clearly. Judy Szink, a reader I'll discuss more below, "wanted to go online and find out all . . . about that wonderful government camp." Other readers, too, offered emphatic approval:

> I liked the social interaction that kind of developed in the camp, the people took on roles that they weren't assigned, but they just kind of emerged out of necessity.[20]
>
> Living in the government camp, how well and how respected they were in those camps and how much the government camps living that way really

> revived their spirits. And how much the people around the area did not want those to succeed.[21]

An even more detailed explication of this idea came in an interview with a retired teacher. Recollecting her childhood in rural Ohio, she described the punishing conditions migrant workers lived in: "dirt floors and no running water." In the 1960s, she noted,

> the government actually stepped in and said you can't have substandard housing. It really took government action. That's a little disheartening. Many things that are right—they don't happen until the government gets in there.

Then turning her personal reflection back to the government camp, she noted, "[The Joads] were taken care of."[22]

The government camp, no doubt, is a key part of the narrative; it is the only stable, institutional solution to the Joads' poverty in the novel. No doubt many readers, then, latched on to the camp as a possible solution to the problem of poverty in 2009. Indeed Jon Hart from CAA, who was instrumental in planning the Services Fair, also noted this scene in discussing the book:

> The government camp that's so well kept, humane. It treats people how you'd want to be treated if you were there. It dispels the idea that poor people are scumbags; it's the system, people are being dehumanized by the system.[23]

But readers don't just remember the camp because it's a heartwarming part of the novel. It sticks in their minds because their local Big Read was organized on a similar principle. The Jackson Services Fair attempts to put these ideals of humane treatment into practice, to provide—on the model of Tom Collins's camps as described in Steinbeck's novel—services to people in poverty without degradation or insult. This mode of reading, then, takes two central chapters from the novel, finds their significance in their description of a workable (if temporary) solution to some specific problems of poverty, and attempts to reproduce this solution in the present.

Yet the Jackson Services Fair also had limits. Attendance was quite low. Only seventy-six people showed up: two-thirds as many as attended the main screening of *Grapes of Wrath*; one-third of the audience of the poetry contest.[24] Perhaps few people attended, as Jessie Murray from CAA put it, because it was "difficult for people to seek help at a public event."[25] This challenge, not incidentally, is predicted by Steinbeck's novel, as when the women's committee insists a woman take five dollars to feed her starving family and she responds "We ain't never took no charity."[26]

Despite this, the Services Fair stands out as an incredibly powerful model for tactical reading. Like the poems I discussed in the previous chapter, it uses literary language in an attempt to shape the way a wide audience thinks about issues of shared concern. It is, perhaps, even more powerful in the way that it shapes not just language but physical space. Tactical readers here use Steinbeck's novel to create spaces where different people interact: those living in poverty, those who work locally with this population, national figures who can help attain governmental support for such efforts. And like the tactical readers I discuss elsewhere in this book, the organizers utilize close attention to Steinbeck's text and work through a process of communicative action to design a space in which the greatest ambition of the novel can be materially realized. Following the example of the Joads, they engage in collaborative work, with the help of (at least partial) government redistribution, to create a space where people in need can get (some of) their needs met.

In this space, links between reading and social justice, between books and politics, and between libraries and social service agencies are made manifest. This mode doesn't just engineer souls to be compassionate or even activist but marshals local power to help people stop foreclosure, get access to social services, or just get a bite to eat. Souls might get engineered along the way, but in the meantime material needs are being served.[27] This is reading as a practice of justice.

Even if this application is limited by low participation, the material benefits delivered show clearly just how powerful it can be. It creates, however briefly, a gathering of people—and a means by which this gathering, with its shared engagements and commitments, can ramify. But such practices are, sadly, not the dominant mode of engagement encouraged by the Big Read. The program focuses on building community in a much more limited sense.

Community: The Big Read and Book Clubs

Above I noted the Big Read's focus on making us "connect with our *communities*"; its mission statement announces that it "encourage[s] reading for pleasure and enlightenment [for] *communities*."[28] Reading, as First Lady Laura Bush put it in a 2007 speech promoting the Big Read, is a key part of "restoring this tight-knit sense of *community*."[29] "Community" is a very important word for the Big Read.

Community, in the Big Read's customary use, is reasonably transparent: it means, as the *OED* puts it, a "body of people who live in the same place"; a town, a city, maybe a county.[30] But it also has a vagueness that trades on the abstract idea of an old-fashioned, "tight-knit" community. That sense, as it happens, exposes some of the problems with "community." In her speech Bush borrows the phrase from *To Kill a Mockingbird* (1960), a book about the sweet, small town community of Maycomb, Alabama. But as the book attests with its focus on race, class, history, and violence, community isn't so simple. To be "tight-knit," often requires "sharing a common cultural or ethnic identity."[31] That addition accounts for the divided community (communities, really) in *To Kill a Mockingbird*. And it also accounts for the Big Read's quasi-subtle rhetoric of racial and ethnic inclusion, which encourages events at "diverse locations involving a wide range of audiences"[32]—important, since the NEA knew well that reading followed various contemporary bright lines of social division: educational, racial, and so on.[33]

The problematic doubleness of community is a familiar theme in attempts to imagine the social world. Critiques of electoral democracy (is it for everyone or just for some?) or nations (are states whole or internally fragmented?) pursue this ambiguity; even critiques of Habermas's public sphere (discussed in the previous chapter) hinge on this problem: is the public sphere really just segregated public spheres? Community—in Jackson and Knoxville as in Maycomb—is really almost always *communities*. To make real changes, you need to find ways to draw those different communities together, across difference, despite conflict. The Big Read (though it never acknowledges the potential divisions in "community") would seem to agree—and its approach (again, somewhat implicit) is that reading is foundational for that project. As Dana Gioia told Congress in 2009, "cultural activities [reading chief among them] seem to awaken a heightened sense of individual awareness and social responsibility."[34] So reading—book clubs in particular—seem to be a foundation for the creation of a community based in "social responsibility." The Big Read, in Gioia's slightly over the top rhetoric, is a shot in the arm for American democracy.

So how do book clubs help create community? They engage people in conversations about literature (and, as any book club member would affirm, about life in general). According to sociologist Elizabeth Long, whose *Book Clubs* (2003) is (surprisingly) among the few scholarly books entirely about this widespread social practice, their benefits are substantial. Studying 121 different book clubs in Houston over the course of nearly a decade, Long concludes that reading and discussing books is "integral to the constitution of both social identity and the sociocultural order" because it can "bring people into new relationships with themselves, each other, and the environing social world."[35] Book clubs lead to self-understanding as well as a better understanding of the world around you. The small body of scholarly work on book clubs echoes this position.[36]

I certainly saw such benefits in my interviews with book club participants. Here are a few particularly rich examples of readers engaging with the novel:

> There were so many things we could connect it to—because it was read at the time when immigration was a big issue. So we had the opportunity to talk about what that means. It was the time when the economy was going down . . . so it was like this had happened before and this is how people had handled it. So the migration of poor people was an issue we discussed and how the people from not only the U.S. but outside of the U.S. migrated just to find a better life. It was very timely—an old book and an old history, but . . . a lot of things that were happening that we could relate to.[37]

> Personally, I loved it. It's the best book I ever read. . . . It was beautiful. Even though it was very depressing. You could just connect with the characters,

even though they weren't anybody I would probably interact with or will ever interact with. You had sympathy, he took you into their world.[38]

I like the book. . . . It really opens your eyes up to what someone in that position has to go through and live through and still try to hold their dignity because it's so degrading.[39]

Empathy is key to these readings ("connect with the characters"; "opens your eyes up to what someone in that position has to go through"), and so is the novel's potential to enrich the reader's understanding of the historical moment ("very timely"; "we could relate"). Another reader, living in transitional housing in Knoxville, claimed the book put her life in perspective. This reader needed no reminder that poverty exists; she had immediate experience. The book, she reported, gave her a positive outlook on her future and her ability to care for herself.[40]

This all harmonizes with the framework I have been using to understand how readers use texts as tactics: people using language in "acts of reaching understanding" that don't just benefit themselves.[41] What's more, reading groups would appear to be ideal incubators of the shared rules by which we think and act and speak about the world.[42] If those rules are being developed in consort with Steinbeck's novel, one can imagine that they would countermand many of the imperatives of late capitalism that led to the Great Recession. The readers above are talking about empathy, not making money. They are thinking about their friends and neighbors before thinking of their own interests.

To this point, let me go a bit deeper with Judy Szink, a reader who exemplifies this type of engagement. Szink, whose praise for the Weedpatch Camp I quoted above, is an upper-middle-class woman who works part time (by choice, not incidentally) for Jackson County, raises three kids, and volunteers with the St. Vincent de Paul Society. She reported to me that she felt the injustice in John Casy's murder and noted that the government camp at Weedpatch is one of the few places in the novel where the Joads exist "at least . . . on a human level." These issues, she made clear, are not just fictional; the novel is "incredibly ripe for the times. Some things you read about in the book are happening right now in current history." Her group discussed "how [*Grapes*] relates to the present day economy and things people were going through," as well as how the current economic situation parallels the 1930s: "there were some greedy people in the 1930s who were able to benefit from what was going on; we think (some of us) that what's going on now is greed and deregulation."[43] Along with this avowedly political—quite radical, really—reading, that "we" is particularly noteworthy, as Szink is speaking for her reading group, acknowledging conflict ("some of us"), but also implying deeper consensus and concern.

The group also helped Szink understand the novel. Initially she was "let down" by the book's ending:

> But then after we discussed it in the book group and with other people subsequent to that, I understood it better and I wasn't so let down then.
>
> I guess I understood the symbolism behind it better; it seems to me that maybe it was the last thing that Rose of Sharon or the family had to give; the only thing they had to give. You still share with someone who needs more than you the last thing you had to give.

This is no simple insight. Overall, she reported it was "a good meeting; conversation flowed," and "everyone had an opinion that day."

This, like the other readings I quote above, is impressive. It's empathetic, but also intellectually complex—seeking deeper understanding of the text, of history, and of our current moment.[44] As a scholar—and as a reader—I am thrilled by such responses.[45] And whether the reader is rich, poor, or somewhere between, empathy for the characters in *Grapes* is important. This is particularly so as, in the readings above, readers link that literary empathy with contemporary experiences of poverty. And while Judy Szink offers a particularly articulate example of this tactical reading, ideas similar to hers showed up in nearly all my interviews.

But Szink's book club practice runs up against a pair of problematic limits related to empathy and community. The first has to do with those whom readers like Szink read with. In *Book Clubs*, Long points out that few book clubs are diverse; despite her large sample, the participants she found were remarkably homogeneous: her readers were *entirely* white, overwhelmingly female (64 percent of her groups were exclusively women), and highly educated (67 percent of her respondents had been to graduate school).[46] Not exactly a representative sample. This tendency toward homogeneity was also clear in my interviews—though even in my small sample I did interview more men and more people of color than did Long. The homogeneity was particularly noteworthy in the nature of these groups. Most participants I met discussed *Grapes* with their accustomed book club, which many reported were made up of people like them: retired teachers, people whose first language is Spanish. And, among these, most of the readers were women, most of them middle-aged.[47]

Though hardly surprising, this homogeneity is still disappointing. But it becomes truly problematic when framed by the Big Read's claims about "community." These homogeneous groups are part of the same "community" only construed in the broadest terms of space and time, not in terms of actual interaction. Book clubs don't knit them together. They just experience similar things in a relatively proximate geography: all the exclusion of community with none of the inclusion.[48]

This helps to explain, I think, the other limit I noticed in my interviews with book clubs: readers recognized problems and empathized with those in need, but most couldn't imagine solutions. So when I reflected back to Judy Szink her ideas about the potential for people to work together to solve problems, she immediately hedged:

> I think that fact hasn't changed, it's just that I think the world is too complex; it's really difficult to effect change because problems and institutions are so big and complex it's hard to just do it on a grassroots level, but it can be done. You have to have passion. I don't know if I have passion, but it can be done. It's just more difficult now than it would've been years ago—because things are more complex.[49]

Suddenly after a conversation about how timely Steinbeck's novel was, Szink pulled back, assigning it to a simpler time in the past, when institutions were less complex, grassroots change more possible.[50] This is precisely what the community organizer, Jon Hart, worried about: a reading that relegates the book to the 1930s, which Szink sees as a time before the rise of complex institutions capable of hindering activism. She couldn't even acknowledge how her work—teaching parenting skills for the county or volunteering with people living in poverty—might be part of an institutional response to inequality.

Book clubs, then, have some clear limits, particularly in the way the interesting and useful emotional and intellectual work they accomplish translates into practice. In these cases, readers read, discuss (sometimes avoiding conflicts),[51] and feel empathy. But that empathy doesn't go beyond the boundary of the book club. So while I am heartened by the responses of these readers, I'm also troubled by the lack of action—whether real or potential—that this type of empathetic, historicizing reading generated. They did not create a newly engaged American democracy; they didn't even establish new links between various segments of their communities. They just affirmed a space where preexisting communities could reconnect. Not a bad thing in itself, but when framed by the Big Read's transformative claims, it's an underwhelming outcome.

And such readings became almost inevitable as I continued my research. Seen in this light, the Big Read's use of "community" and "social responsibility" certainly looks somewhat unconvincing. Empathy, a clarified relationship with oneself, connections to people like you, a recognition of one's historical position—these things matter, but they are not in themselves political or even necessarily politicizing. They might make people feel things for others, but community is not created by such feelings alone.

I want to pause here to note that the Big Read is hardly alone, among other contemporary modes of civic engagement, in its evocation of vague political impacts on an ill-defined community. In avoiding more clearly defined political outcomes—not mentioning recognition, representation, redistribution; not seeming to imagine the possible need for structural change—the Big Read has much in common with service learning and many facets of the "civic engagement" movement on college campuses that I'll discuss more in chapters 3 and 4. But for now, I want to stick with Dana Gioia's claims about (a rather anodyne) "social responsibility" and compare those to Steinbeck's more precise definition of dignity as "a register of a [human's] responsibility to the community." In that clear contrast we can recognize something more effectual happening: practices of everyday politics that promote justice and transcend the limited, historical horizons of many existing communities. Such are the possibilities illuminated by these tactical readers.

Communal Reading

The power of people to work together is the foundational idea of *The Grapes of Wrath*. While often described as "the story of one Oklahoma farm family," the novel is more emphatically the story of many people coming together along much less traditional lines than "family" or a state of origin. From the partnership in the second chapter between Tom Joad and the nameless truck driver to the famous final scene, just referred to by Judy Szink, where Rose of Sharon offers her breast to save the life of an unnamed stranger, the book explores ways of working together.[52] Families disperse and are re-created in ways traditional (Tom's moving reunion with his parents and siblings) and less so (Jim Casy's adoption of the Joads, the extended families created at the boxcar encampment); strangers struggle together (the Joads and the Wilsons support each other through death and illness on the road; travelers point others to water or a good campsite) and strive to improve one another (as with Al Joad and Floyd Knowles's collaboration on engine work; as with the one-eyed junkyard attendant whom Tom, a bit brutally, tries to empower). The list could go on—at least between the covers of the novel. But are such connections realistic in America in the early twenty-first century? Is it even possible for people to gather together? Aren't we just, in Robert Putnam's apt phrase, bowling alone, making whatever connections we can via Facebook over the wireless from our techno-foxholes?[53]

So if hundreds, thousands—even millions, really—of people read *Grapes* in their book clubs and develop ideas at odds with hyperindividualized late capitalist culture, the political value of this work would nonetheless merit some doubt. Such ideas might sprout in familiar gatherings (often in private places), but how will they take root in such inhospitable cultural soil? To claim book clubs are politically effective, then, not only overstates the consequences of conversations but misunderstands the nature of political action itself, particularly in America in the early twenty-first century. Democracy in discussion is all well and good, but is not necessarily productive of democracy in practice.

Here's where tactical readings, like the Jackson Services Fair, come into play. While they have a lot in common with book clubs, they are quite different in what they accomplish. Tactical readers not only encourage ideas about connecting with others, but they actually work to build readers' organizational capacities to create such connections on a large scale. This concluding section documents how they do so.

Like book clubs, tactical reading develops language and ideas about connection and mutual support. But unlike book clubs, tactical reading puts language and ideas into action by working to produce immediate material benefits. The fair explicitly works for the empowerment of those currently living in poverty through a combination of self-directed collective action and governmental support structures. The difference from a book club is huge: it's the difference between talking about how it's important to feed people and putting lunch in people's hands while helping them learn where they could get lunch tomorrow. Both approaches might be marked by empathy, but tactical reading puts empathy into practice. This is the responsibility to others Steinbeck writes about. Whether you're an organizer, someone staffing a booth, or someone coming to learn about benefits, you have to cross divisions—and in a nonhierarchical way. You are meeting others, some of whom are quite different from you, and are working together to make it easier for everyone to live. This is radically inclusive in a way a book club can't be. How do you invite a stranger to your book club when you don't know her? And it also shifts the idea of community to something more collective by making the single prerequisite for membership an active choice: the choice to read (or, as in Cummings's *Citizen Patriot* story, to be curious about reading) Steinbeck's novel.

The Services Fair is, without doubt, the strongest example I can provide of such a collective practice. But such nonhierarchical collectivities—diverse in gender, race, class, age, and, crucially, relations to literature—appeared elsewhere in Jackson and in Knoxville.

Knoxville hosted the Mayor's Book Club, a well-attended lunch-hour discussion of *Grapes* (which also aired multiple times on local television). Moderated by Knoxville mayor Mike Ragsdale (and you might want to pause there for a moment: the mayor of a city of more than a million people hosting a book club in real life and on TV; it really happened), the discussion included other local politicians, members of the Hispanic Chamber of Commerce, high school students, and religious leaders. Among other things, Mayor Ragsdale said, "We talked . . . about our favorite characters, how [the book] could make us better public servants, and what we're seeing in today's economic situation."[54]

The program helped one viewer understand the book in a different way: "the fact that they tied into today what was happening years ago. . . . I thought that was very interesting."[55] On the surface, this is not a remarkable analysis. But the woman who told me this had recently relocated to Knoxville because of financial difficulties. She clearly recognized echoes of her own experience in the book. So her statement here would seem to be directed more at how "interesting" (i.e., important) it is to see politicians (and the others on stage) recognizing (remember this word from the previous chapter?) her experience. Looking at it from a different perspective, another reader—a longtime resident with a stable job and life—noted that "if our leaders are reading, they're just going to be more reflective, have better perspective, and be better leaders."[56]

Such acts of literary interpretation performed by elected representatives are noteworthy because they, as these readers indicate, say something about the core principle of representative democracy. These readers who aren't politicians are seeing politicians doing something like they are (reading the book) and using it to reflect on experiences both like, and unlike, their own. This recognition—and I mean the word in the philosophical sense—by elected representatives is further emphasized by the fact that this isn't just a campaign speech, but a discussion in which elected officials share the lectern with retirees and teenagers, to say nothing of people from different countries of origin or different classes. This not only broadens the notion of what the community is, but draws different communities into a more actively produced and shared notion of responsibility. At this level, then, tactical readings amplify the shared ideas and symbols at the core of these communities but also work to produce communal bonds around these ideas and symbols: they make manifest the ideas expressed in language.[57] And this can happen only because events like the Mayor's Book Club take place in ways that open them to a range of publics.

Another example of tactical reading would be the two sermons delivered by Rev. Dr. Cynthia Landrum, the minister of the Universalist Unitarian Church of East Liberty in Jackson. In the first, she reads Steinbeck's novel as a parable about "the importance and value of anger" in response to layoffs and bank bailouts, executive salaries, and medical debt. The book, she argues, is both a rejection of "absolute capitalism, trickle-down, American dream" and a reclamation of "the inherent worth and dignity of every person."[58] The next week Landrum's sermon linked this message to local layoffs (described by industry and closing date) and the skyrocketing unemployment rate, particularly its racial dynamics (in Jackson—as in much of the United States—disproportionately affecting African Americans). Then she argued that social justice is the foundational belief of her Unitarian Universalist congregation, pushing them to act on their anger.

Along with her sermon, which, echoing the Services Fair, urged her audience to link reading and action, Landrum encouraged her congregation members to share their own interpretations. After church, she shifted from minister to book group leader, opening the church's common room for a more general discussion of *Grapes*: "We talked about the economy now. What about Steinbeck is relevant to our experience? People really got in-depth about that. In ways that surprised me. It connected very strongly."[59] Given that her flock had just heard two sermons about the reality of poverty in their immediate community, it's not at all surprising to me that the novel connected.

Along with focusing her congregation on the novel, Landrum also discussed *Grapes* with other populations. In particular, she worked with community members in planning a forum called "The Face of Poverty in Jackson: A Call to Action." Officially one of the church's outreach events, its "CommUnity ForUms" (the double "U" is for Universalist Unitarian) are held at the downtown library once a month. While they do have spiritual aspects, they often address questions of a more material nature. March's forum—co-organized with the Big Read's planning committee—was dedicated to the question of what it means "to be really poor in America" and to "multiple aspects of the causes of and solutions for poverty."[60] The panel was hosted by Landrum and Jon Hart of CAA, who is also a member of Landrum's congregation. Some of the audience, of course, were Unitarians who'd heard Landrum's sermons. But the more than forty people in attendance represented a diverse slice of Jackson, as audiences for "forUms" have since 2007, when the town was reading *To Kill a Mockingbird* for the Big Read. That year's CommUnity ForUm, cosponsored with the NAACP, drew a large crowd and spawned Jackson Justice Watch, a group of citizens dedicated to identifying and eliminating racism in Jackson.

The Mayor's Book Club and Cynthia Landrum's work, from her sermons to the CommUnity ForUm, echo aspects of the Services Fair. All militate against the isolated or passive interpretive practices of book clubs. All bring together diverse collectives outside of familiar spaces; and all are, by design, primed to focus on interpretation as a precursor to action.[61] The organizers, recognizing that it's hard to rebuild community around separate gatherings with finite spatial and temporal limits, have tried hard to engage a wider audience.

Indeed, this is the second feature that marks tactical readings as distinct from book clubs: they create linkages between smaller, limited publics. The multiple audiences that Cynthia Landrum engaged in reading would be an obvious example of this. While each setting—the sermons, the church book club, the CommUnity ForUm—doesn't pursue precisely the same idea or discussion, for those who attend all, the repetition serves to develop or enforce the ideas. And for those who attend just one, they are linked with those who have attended other iterations in this shared interpretive practice. As I note above, Landrum uses a commitment to social justice to draw together both her Unitarian congregation and others with similar commitments. The Mayor's Book Club includes (and because of this encourages attention from) people both young and old, people involved in the immigration debate and people who might know nothing about it.

Faces of Poverty, Kate Lambert Lee's photography exhibit, offers another example of the capacity of tactical readings to connect multiple audiences. It was a key part of the Services Fair and was subsequently shuttled around to other major events in Jackson during the month of the Big Read. Its name, you may have noticed, appears in the CommUnity ForUm's title, too ("The Face of Poverty in Jackson: A Call to Action.") Big Read records indicate hundreds of people saw it; and its presence in the library, in the high school, and elsewhere surely stirred conversations similar to those happening at the Services Fair.

Faces also made a trip to Washington, DC. The head of Jackson's Community Action Agency, testifying before Congress in 2009, "brought these documents to talk about the people in the community."[62] The collection of images and stories of people living in (and in proximity to) poverty in Jackson serves to remind those in Jackson and those in Washington, DC, what's at stake—even if the viewer sees the images only on the library wall as she passes by on her way to check out a Muppets DVD.

Other installations were similarly designed to connect and engage multiple audiences. One, in the Knoxville YWCA's transitional housing facility, promoted the Big Read by linking the Joads' migration narrative with another Depression-era experience (one notably absent from Steinbeck's novel): urban, multiracial poverty. Angela Cash, who worked at the front desk, produced a bulletin board that included copies of pictures she found at the library: "some pictures with soup kitchens [with] all these men [who] came from different backgrounds . . . : Italian, Caucasian, black" and pictures of "residential areas [that] look like dumping grounds where these people live."[63]

These tactical readings expand the temporal and spatial frame of mass, public reading practices. Even in the absence of an immediate gathering, they work to create a larger and more responsive community. They do this not only by pursuing the themes present in other tactical readings—empathy, the need for structural change to eliminate poverty—but by pushing Steinbeck's text in new directions (gently critiquing it, we might say) to include not just the plight of "Okies" or migrants, not just the struggles of white people.

In these ways, tactical readings effectively bring people together while critically making claims for recognition and political representation —presenting the faces and voices of people living in poverty to governmental representatives as well as to their neighbors; announcing the way race and poverty intersect and resisting the all-too-familiar erasure of the experiences of poor urban African Americans during the Depression. Material objects like Cash's bulletin board and Lambert Lee's photos demand recognition and represent the unrepresentable.[64]

Tactical readings, I'm trying to emphasize, link readers: first, literally by putting them in the same room, as in the Services Fair; then, through a kind of reduplicative property. The ideas from the Services Fair show up in other practices—like Landrum's sermons, like the poetry contest, like community conversations about the Civilian Conservation Corps. So the most successful tactical practices echo in other public reading practices. The echo of tactical readings is amplified by the tangible objects—the photos, the displays, the repeat performances or multiple showings—that further encourage a shared interpretive practice beyond discrete gatherings. If you saw Kate Lambert Lee's photos or Angela Cash's bulletin board, you interpreted the book differently in your own private reading than someone who didn't. If two people in your book club saw them, they could easily become part of that conversation.

I've been highlighting the distinction between tactical readings and book clubs, but here's the link: tactical readings can shape conversations in the more prosaic and private sphere of book clubs. Tactical readings provide a link between these isolated interpretations; they operate as a kind of connective tissue.[65] Tactical readings create mass public gatherings. And for those who can't attend, they percolate into the community not only through general conversations but through the Big Read's ancillary events, like a film screening, an installation, or a lecture. They speak even to people who might not have finished (or even read) the book.[66]

You could see these public, tactical readings as working linguistically to shape interpretive frames (suggesting that people should read "politically" and link what they read to the present) and more materially to connect such interpretation and social practice. There's an elegant recursivity in that: tactical readings help people work together while encouraging them to endorse the notion that people need to work together to solve problems. And each aspect of these interpretive practices reinforces the others. This was visible even at the level of conversation. As one organizer in Knoxville put it, reading brought "this diverse group together to talk about something they'd never under any normal circumstances talk about."

> The way they talked about the book and society and all these issues that came up—the way they treated each other in the discussion . . . I felt like was partially a result of having read that book and being moved by that "working together, depending on each other" theme.[67]

This multistage process of connecting people from shared reading to shared interpretation and, ultimately, shared commitment to change is how the organizers created something more than "community," in its limited, traditional sense. Like the fictional camp, these real world connections, too, came up again and again in interviews. Without tactical readings, one white woman asked me,

> How would I meet a forty- or fifty-year-old black woman on the south side and end up spending time? You know, it brought people together that wouldn't normally meet.[68]

Said another, "I've talked with people I've never seen before. It was kind of neat to meet people—new people I've never seen before. I really enjoy getting others' input."[69] A third reader didn't talk about meeting strangers but went into detail about how she had "developed a really good relationship" with someone with shared interests, how she had "strengthen[ed] [her] friendship" with another acquaintance, and even how the program helped her "reconnect to a girl [she] went to high school with."[70]

Such new and developing relationships were happening at institutional levels as well—for instance, between Knoxville's county library system, the YWCA, and a literacy nonprofit in a neighboring county. Those connections might have ramifications in many contexts. People, as in the quotes above, got to know people they didn't know before: it sounds simple, but really is no small feat in our atomized and segregated country. To put it another way, whether or not readers in Jackson were at the Services Fair, they benefitted from it. Even if a reader didn't attend the Mayor's Book Club in Knoxville, she felt its reverberations. Tactical reading created active engagement among people and a shared sense of responsibility to others who were sometimes similar (but unknown) and sometimes quite different from them; it enabled, in other words, recognition. Tactical reading also engaged in redistribution, particularly of immediate material needs. While it is perhaps more remarkable that a book could be used to organize people to deliver services to those in need, this power to connect diverse people—to build organizational capacity—is the ultimate guarantor of the collective's political potential.

Despite all this, many of the tactical readers, as I've noted, still saw the limits they faced. One particularly dour assessment came from the Reverend Cynthia Landrum. Evoking the foreclosure crisis and connecting it to the brutal interchapter in *Grapes* that describes the destruction of food to maintain artificially high prices—kerosene poured over oranges, coffee burned for fuel, pigs killed and left to putrefy—she told me: "We need the Steinbeck for our era to emerge."[71] In a way, her concern is justified. The work of the tactical readers in Knoxville and Jackson had limits. Then again, the practices I've been describing fostered not only immediate benefits but an incredible potential. While these collectivities came together around the oasis of Big Read grant support, once the money has dried up and the reports have been filed, the newly created communities remain, even if dormant. The connections persist, whether in conversations about applying for next year's Big Read or conversations among new acquaintances founded on these collective ideals.[72]

It's easy to speculate about the continuation and development of the collectivities shaped by these practices, both institutional and personal. Even readers who did not speak during the Big Read, maybe did not even read *Grapes of Wrath*, now have something—new words, new characters, new narratives, new ideas, new practices—that enables communication and more effective coordination around shared political goals. So perhaps when people come together in another context, at a school board or town council meeting or at a protest, they may deploy the shared grammar developed in these tactical reading practices.

But I have to emphasize that because these practices are tactical, not strategic, not controlled by one institution, party, or person, they may sprout in unexpected ways. Tactics, grounded in this shared grammar, are capable of responding to changing circumstances "in an infinite variety of ways."[73] This adaptable, radically democratic approach is in no small part where their power comes from. And that adaptability, of course, helps these practices spread beyond local networks, as well. The willingness of tactical readers in Jackson and Knoxville to bring me into their networks has led to my broadcasting (in the literal sense) of their work. While I haven't been to Jackson or Knoxville since 2009, the ideas folks there developed have become part of my own research and writing, spread as I've been blown by the winds of the academic job market from Minnesota to Oregon, spread as I've talked about them at conferences around the country, spread as I've worked with community organizations in Portland. And spread, too, among my students, the topic of the next chapter.

To some, that will sound overly sunny—practitioners of community-based scholarship are often accused of naïve optimism.[74] But having met these tactical readers, it's hard not to be hopeful. So, sure, I'd be happy for another Steinbeck to write a *Grapes of Wrath* for contemporary America. But what I saw in Jackson and Knoxville was something far more powerful than the work of one writer.

3

Talking with Strangers about Working-Class Literature

against service learning

The women get on the train. The shorter one, her pregnancy just starting to show, is clutching a stack of questionnaires. The other, only slightly taller, has a huge backpack and her black ponytail hangs almost to her waist. As the train starts out of the station, they pause before the tall one heads for the man mashed into the seat at the farthest end of the car. The other woman follows. After quiet introductions, Tarale begins to ask him questions while Eleshia tries to record his answers. As the train shudders into a tunnel, both women reach out for balance.

In the small kitchen, three classmates are clustered around a laptop. Two—flip-flops and shorts; smart phones in hand—might be students on any college campus in the United States. The third, Sheree, could be their mom. Her hair, graying, is pulled back in a tight bun; one finger holds her place in a hardback book wrapped in an interlibrary loan (ILL) sleeve. Other books, many in matching ILL sleeves, are scattered over the table and on her bedspread. Addison clicks through century-old pictures of men clear-cutting forests and laughs as Lindsay tries to explain what exactly a Tumblr is.

By now, you recognize them: people using texts as tactics. And Addison, Lindsay, Sheree, Tarale, and Eleshia do have many similarities to those readers I've examined in the previous chapters: they use reading to bring people together and, as I'll show, to engage in everyday politics. But their inclusion in this book also signals a turn. While the first two chapters resolutely take literature off college campuses—focusing on those publics that traditional scholars have mostly ignored—*Reading as Collective Action* was written *on* college campuses and participates in conversations happening predominately on those campuses, among the publicly engaged scholars who have participated in similar work and, to a lesser extent, in literary studies.

Indeed, my turn back to campus shares the logic of much contemporary thinking about "engagement" today; it allows me, as a professor, to link research and teaching while producing some mutual benefits for both communities—those on campus and beyond.[1] And even outside the frame of public engagement, campuses are well-known incubators of political work: think of the Student Nonviolent Coordinating Committee and, more recently, antisweatshop campaigns.[2] I won't speculate here about why and how (familiar explanations like the Marxist professoriate probably don't cover it). But it is clear that even in this era of defunding and retrenchment, even in the sadly STEM-less humanities, campuses do have institutional surpluses (of time, money, and prestige) that can help support tactical reading practices—and not just support them, but actually teach them.

College campuses are without doubt one key place where people read literature today and also a key place where people *learn to read* literature; thus influencing how people on campuses read has a potentially wide impact. So while this book's first two chapters have traced the use of literature in mostly nonacademic contexts—from newspapers to community meetings, from About.com to transitional housing facilities—the classroom has to be seen as another site in these struggles. For all those reasons, this chapter pursues the pedagogy of texts as tactics. It starts out by narrating an assignment from one of my literature courses and, in the second and third sections, describes the work the students you just met produced in response to it. I chose these examples because they were particularly impressive, though certainly of the same species as many of the projects produced by their peers.

Once I decided to write about *Rough Crossing* and Tarale and Eleshia's interview project, I sat down for informal interviews with these readers, who were no longer my students. (The only one I missed was Eleshia; she had her baby the summer after she took the class.) They were excited to share the parts of their work that had been invisible to me in my instructor role. And as my own project has dragged through peer review, Lindsay and Sheree have both kept asking if this book will ever come out.

Describing the assignment, the projects, and how these students subsequently felt about them, I am also, of course, writing about my own attempts to create a pedagogy shaped not by familiar disciplinary practices—e.g., close reading; more on that in chapter 4—but by public engagement. As you'll see, the pedagogical work here, in ways not always clear to students, uses the ideas and practices of the tactical readers whose work makes up the previous chapters. With their help, I step into the critical conversation around perhaps the best-known example of public engagement on and off college campuses: service learning. The fourth section situates this assignment in that context. While I acknowledge many similarities with thinkers who have critiqued traditional service learning as incapable of fomenting real political change, I also hold so-called critical service learning up for critique. By linking contemporary scholarship on political engagement in higher education with the political ideas I've discussed throughout, I argue that—particularly for literature courses—projects teaching students to use texts as tactics are more effective at encouraging both immediate political action and students' long-term organizational capacities.

So while this is a chapter about pedagogy and on-campus discussions, it is, like the preceding chapters, also a document of how people use texts as tactics to engage in acts of recognition, representation, and redistribution. I'm studying students not as students, but as political actors working for a more just world.

The Assignment

A few years ago, I wrote an article arguing that teaching, even teaching political subjects, is not inherently political. I argued that the classroom —and its complicity in structures of oppression: admissions policies, seating arrangements, grades—is rarely a site for activism.[3] It felt a bit like an admission of failure. But I didn't give up thinking about how to make my classroom more activist.

When I began teaching at Portland Community College, I found a course on the books that seemed well suited to pursuing these questions: American Working Class Literature. Years ago a now-retired colleague created the course and named it.[4] I have preferred to advertise my classes under the title "Occupy Literature," in large part just to get students in the door.[5] But, making history under the conditions I've inherited, I do use the course's title to push the boundaries of "America" (a nation-state? A region? A set of exploitative economic relationships?) and to explore the limits of "working-class" identity: we read about sex workers and people without homes; undocumented kitchen workers; and, yes, white, male manual laborers.

This is heavy work in a room speckled with pre-major literature readers and a handful of students with deep political commitments but mostly folks who are intrigued by the title or just looking for a four-credit course that fits their schedule. Each year, we have fights about whether Americans even recognize class—and I give a lecture explaining (justifying?) the prevalence of socialism in our readings. Despite these challenges, I felt this class offered me a good chance to develop an assignment that would make teaching more about enabling activism by encouraging students to use texts as tactics. After all, many of the texts we read are radical in themselves; so they seem promising catalysts to turn reading into something more than the gathering of good stories or interesting bits of long-ago history.[6] The assignment I'll describe here is my best—though, of course, always under revision—attempt at this synthesis of pedagogy and politics.

In the spring of 2014, I framed the students' final assignment like this: "*What I Really, Really Want: I want you to think about working-class literature and its place in the world.*" As it said at the top of the assignment,

> This project asks you to put our work into practice—or at least imagine how you might. You will publish a piece of literature that corresponds with *your* definition of working-class literature. Publishing the text means making it public—perhaps through performance, reading, video adaptation, a lecture, presentation, demonstration, open letter or . . . something else.[7]

Those examples—very few of which students took up—were widely varied with the intention of suggesting the project's openness. To mollify the legitimate terror produced by such a wide-open assignment, I gave the students three frameworks: (1) to imagine, (2) to imagine and do, and (3) to create. The first asked them to "imagine a publication strategy for an already existing piece of work." In this version, students would write up a plan for how they might (re)publish a text we'd read in the course (or some other text they deemed "working-class") with an aim toward particular political consequences. The second option—imagine and do—was the approach I was pushing for; the nudge (not very subtle, I admit) was that they would have to write much less.[8] Their main work, beyond imagining how to (though I didn't call it this) use texts as tactics, was to document their labor with photos or videos or a short narrative. The third option—create—allowed students to produce a piece of working-class literature in one of their preferred genres.

While I really wanted students to "imagine and do," I thought it important to include the other choices, mainly because of the diversity of the community college population. I'm inspired by amazing assignments like those by Kathryn Miles, whose Unity College literature students engage in an act of civil disobedience for their final project, and Kara Mollis, whose students study women's novels, then work to fix the injustices they find there; but in translating those approaches to my college, I saw some structural limits.[9] Creative, collaborative projects require not just lots of time, but flexible time: some of Miles's students rode hundreds of miles on their bikes to lobby against genetically modified foods, for instance. Many of my students do their homework on the bus home after a shift at their second job that ends after midnight—not exactly a collaborative space. For them imagining an intervention seemed to come close to the spirit of the project, even if it wasn't an actual political intervention.[10]

I announced the assignment on the first day of the term. And, as weeks passed, we discussed the project both in the context of other assignments and of our readings. So when, for instance, students turned in a formal essay about how they would define working-class literature, I reminded them that this definition probably should shape how they thought about their project. When they generated a playlist of working-class songs, we talked about how these songs could (or couldn't) work as different versions of this assignment.

Throughout the term, we examined not only texts but the contexts of their varied uses. We looked at Langston Hughes, whose poem "Let America Be America Again" (1936) has been republished by everyone from the International Workers Order to John Kerry during his 2004 presidential run. One term, as we read *Grapes of Wrath,* we discussed Steinbeck's use of different genres—fiction, journalism, correspondence with Eleanor Roosevelt—to bring the plight of the migrants to wider awareness, as well as the politicizing (or depoliticizing) adaptations of his work in John Ford's film and Ricky Ian Gordon's recent *Grapes* opera. I also told them about what the folks in Jackson and Knoxville you met in chapter 2 had done with the book. (Again, these practices fold back in on themselves.) Another term, we talked about why Tillie Olsen didn't finish *Yonnondio* (1974) and how a writer might conceive of her organizing work as more important than finishing a novel. We looked at actual publications—labor publications; videos of Occupy encampment slam poetry; the radio stations where working-class songs they selected had (or hadn't) played.

The course, in other words, thought about the creation of literature in an iteratively materialist paradigm: not just the conditions under which it was created and published or the moment of initial publication but also, to echo my reading of Marx at the end of the first chapter here, how literature becomes part of the way humans "make their own history" not "just as they please in circumstances they choose for themselves; rather . . . in present circumstances, given and inherited."[11] To put it in more literary-critical terms, we didn't just focus on New Criticism (what the text says) or biographical or new historicist approaches (who wrote it or how it came to be written). We tried to discover texts as tactics.

The more we discussed how others had used texts as tactics, the more this approach began to shape the students' thinking about the assignment. I was asking them to do only what so many others before them had done, after all. In dialogue with students, I emphasized the links between our readings and discussions and their developing projects. In each instance, I encouraged them to focus on the big theme—making literature public, using, in my language here, texts as tactics—not the assignment's particulars. So lots of students blended elements of the three options: one created a kind of annotated table of contents for an anthology of working-class women writers he wanted to edit; another revised the lyrics from the IWW's *Little Red Song Book* (1909) to reflect more inclusive ideas about gender, race, and sexuality; one combined her own poetry with links to other working-class poets in a blog; another made a video with images of dustbowl migrants, soundtracked by his metal band playing a song inspired by *The Grapes of Wrath*.[12] Others have performed songs for our class, illustrated scenes from novels we've read, organized film screenings; the variety of projects is fascinating.[13]

The point of the assignment was to help students conceptualize literature as part of social action—as a connector, a mode of representation, a redistributive agent, a way to have an impact within and beyond their most immediate network. It was to make students see how texts could be tactics. But it was also to make them recognize their own agency as tacticians. They were not just studying the political labors of past radicals with transformative agendas. They were becoming them.

Tarale and Eleshia: Literature and Class Consciousness

Before they got on the train, Tarale and Eleshia (*Tara*—like the plantation—*lee*; *Eleshia*—both *e*'s are long) had done a lot of work. They had met in a previous course and signed up for this class together. For this project, they decided they wanted to understand what other people thought of working-class literature. They took the assignment I had given them earlier in the term—to create their own definition—and, in essence, assigned it to strangers. The idea itself is an act of reappropriation, taking my power as assignment-maker and making it their own.

When they first told me they wanted to interview people, I was surprised. This kind of action research, challenging to most everyone, seemed particularly challenging to two women who were fairly quiet in class. Balancing my desire to be their cheerleader with my desire that they not get yelled at by strangers on account of my class, I warned them that trying to convince people on the train to talk about class and literature was a bold project. Tarale reassured me that she had worked many jobs—from construction to advertising for stores by flipping signs next to busy streets all day; she knew what she was getting into. So we talked a little about *Distinction* (1984) and Pierre Bourdieu's research methods, and they left my office.

The project ultimately took the idea of making our work *public* in a very real way. They planned to ride the MAX trains from the stop near our college, at the border of exurban sprawl and sprawling farmland, to downtown and back. They would have public conversations on public transit,[14] asking questions about people's jobs (or lack thereof), their pay and benefits, their understanding of class, and (finally) their ideas of a good working-class song or book. This was remarkable work—especially for a literature course. I was excited, if still a bit worried.

They not only survived but in just a few weeks managed to interview fifty-six people—far more than I would've imagined possible. And some of the small details they recorded were fascinating: who knew Ayn Rand and Bruno Mars were working-class artists? But the results, at that granular level, were not what I found interesting.[15] For Tarale and Eleshia, the consequences were substantial. They were proud of what they'd accomplished, while acknowledging room for improvement: both used phrases like "far more complicated than I'd anticipated" in their reflections. They had pushed themselves, not just intellectually, but socially, breaking through their admitted reluctance to approach interviewees at various points and ultimately recognizing the benefits of this risk: "I did enjoy actually talking to people, hearing their responses, learning where they worked, and what they thought. Even if I didn't understand it, it was interesting to hear their responses."

These conversations illustrated—in, I suspect, a new way for Tarale and Eleshia—the real connections and tensions between what happens on campus and what happens in the rest of the world. As they learned, the term "class," if not particularly conflict producing in our classroom, was a different story on the MAX.[16] Some interviewees rejected the framing—either legitimately misunderstanding the terms (like "class consciousness"; more on that in a moment) or feigning ignorance to avoid a discussion. In (at least) one case, the women reported a particularly virulent response: "I feel bad for people, but I don't think taxing the rich is the answer" (given, Tarale and Eleshia pointedly note, by the highest earner in their sample). On the other hand, they write, "An interesting fact to note: all six of the people who said they were part of a union also said they liked their job." This was "interesting" because we had explored the roles of unions in building a better life for the working class in our discussions. Much of what they heard, in other words, comported with what we had studied.

In analyzing their sample, they noted many similarities to our in-class work, but they chose to focus on a key disconnect. The report dwells mostly on the tension in their interviewees' responses to the question about class consciousness. While half of those interviewed "simply said they didn't care, or that they never thought about it," the researchers note that many interviewees could easily say whether or not they were from a working-class family. "Over all, [the question about class consciousness] seemed to make most people surveyed uncomfortable," perhaps because, as these students reported,

> Class consciousness, being aware of your position in society, is not enough to get a rise out of people. Even the few people who said that things had to change sounded as though it was expected of them. Though every one of them was working-class, they didn't seem to feel a connection with their fellow workers, or a true need to do anything about it. They just didn't care.
>
> People today have been made complacent. This is how things are, and with so many things to distract them, they're not going to rise up into a rebellion for change. It just isn't important enough to them. They're more concerned with their own lives, their own comforts, the next big thing.

This analysis aligns with the work of many scholars about the enchantments of consumer culture and the decline of working-class power in America.[17] It also echoes Judy Szink, from the last chapter, who lamented the impossibility of change today. But, while the insight is not, in this sense, groundbreaking, that it comes from their own field research (not just the library) enhances—politically and intellectually—its value.

They were no longer students doing the work assigned to them by filling in check boxes on a rubric; by virtue of their approach, they had taken on the role of experts doing their own research. In this, they tested not only themselves—as thinkers and researchers—but also many of the ideas we had been discussing in class. Both their successful research and their insights are closely related to the role the project encouraged them to take on. Their deployment of texts as tactics left them intellectually empowered.[18] That intellectual power is clear in how they use their report not just to critique some of their interviewees, but to argue with our course's readings (their research "gives the lie" to hopeful books like *Grapes of Wrath,* they note) and, perhaps less directly, their instructor. And however sorrowful it is for me to read such bleak insights, they are certainly the stuff of education, both (again) intellectual and political.

This experience crystallizes—at the college level—Paolo Freire's well-known ambition to develop student-teachers and teacher-students, where "they become jointly responsible for the process in which all grow."[19] Indeed, as Freire's theory posits, their intellectual empowerment supported these new political insights. These women had, at the most basic level, pronounced the words "working class" to a bunch of strangers on a train. To talk about class, much less class consciousness, in America in the early twenty-first century—at a time when even vaguely redistributionist policies are labeled "Socialism"—and to do so with strangers is the essence of everyday politics. Just by asking the questions of their interviewees they were shaping language and (often) both directly and indirectly defining terms of conversation. And even though some of the answers they received from their interlocutors were dismissive or classist, Eleshia and Tarale remained engaged—no cable news–style shouting matches here. These encounters in so many ways exemplify a speech situation often described as impossible in early twenty-first century America;[20] yet here it was enacted by two students and a bunch of strangers on trains rushing through Portland's western suburbs.

Addison, Lindsay, and Sheree: *Rough Crossing*

Earlier I described Sheree, Addison, and Lindsay in the midst of creating *Rough Crossing*, a Tumblr documenting working-class life.[21] Each of *Rough Crossing*'s fifteen pages features an early-twentieth-century image, some with poetry or prose superimposed. Though eclectic, the collection places some emphasis on logging in the Pacific Northwest. The layout—a dim, gray-brown background, headed with a strip of maroon—draws attention to the images, which themselves appear as part of pages in a steno notebook (a reporter's notes? a symbolic gesture to the group's archival process?). The layout is serious, and the pages do not flicker with ads or the other detritus that often comes with free websites.[22]

The pages are not ordered into a chronology or narrative, but the site still feels coherent. One slide features Dorothea Lange's famous *Migrant Mother* image, with three lines from Lucia Trent's "Breed, Women, Breed" (1929) superimposed: "Breed, little mothers / Breed for the owners of mills / And the owners of mines." Below the image the group placed the full text of the poem. Another image—much less well known—shows loggers working to bring down a gigantic Douglas fir and includes the fatalistic quatrain titled the "Logger's Lullaby":

> I eat when I'm hungry
> I drink when I'm dry
> If a tree don't fall on me
> I'll live till I die.

This page has more reblogs and comments than any other, except for a similar image that includes even more lumberjacks standing in a tremendous notch they've hacked into the body of another massive fir. Another page matches an image of the Triangle Shirtwaist Factory with Tillie Olsen's "I Want You Women Up North to Know" (1934). On another, text condemning the lack of access to culture ("Did you ever see a sign in the working class district pointing the way to the public library?") sits over an image of men gathered around an oil-drum fire in front of the Tacoma Commons Mission.

It's a strong collection. The words, powerful in themselves, are often more so with the images. While many of the texts are well known—Trent's poem, Tess Gallagher's "Black Money" (1976), Wobbly Rayfield Becker's famous quip that "Christ was a Tramp"—the students collected all of it on their own; nothing here was assigned reading. And it was cobbled together from a range of resources that are hardly easy to access. Indeed, as Sheree, who had come back to school in her fifties, initially just to work on computer skills, wrote in her reflection, the research was extensive:

> This opened up a whole new world for me and I began to learn so much more than I had ever imagined regarding the working class, labor unions, authors and organizers. So many people worked tirelessly through these times to bring equality to the work force, recognition of working conditions to the public and fair wages to the working class. . . . I found hundreds of photos shot during these troubled times and culled what were some of the best for the website.

Indeed, each of the students describes finding more material than they could accommodate; all mention the work of Anise, whose blend of activism and radical modernism made a real impression on them. Though her poems don't appear in *Rough Crossing*, she is given a nod on the hyperlinked "Citations Page"—really a bibliography—that allows the group to include some of their surplus. Along with Anise, the page features some academic tomes, including Cary Nelson's *Repression and Recovery* and Charlotte Nekola and Paula Rabinowitz's *Writing Red: An Anthology of American Women Writers* (1987).[23]

So while, yes, Lange's image is beyond famous and the Rayfield Becker quote is well known, these students, like Tarale and Eleshia, created something of their own. This is perhaps most obvious in the mixing of media and the organization of the Tumblr. But behind the scenes, their work involved not only building a bibliography but growing the limited web-accessible archive of working-class culture by keying in undigitized texts. This isn't just a term paper—proof that they did the reading but sadly destined to live on only in a file drawer. This is real work, scholarly and creative, that exists in the world.[24]

As they brought *Rough Crossing* online, the trio also promoted it both digitally, via online blasts on social media and to our class, and in the nondigital world, using posters that teased images from the site with QR codes to drive traffic. Within a few days of going online, the page had more than two hundred hits. (A year later, it has more than six hundred.) While this doesn't compare to the stratospheric traffic driven by funny cat videos, it's no small number for a site that is resolutely serious and promotes not only a version of history that has been repressed (or, when acknowledged, shrugged off) but a radical way of seeing that history. On *Rough Crossing*, lumberjacks aren't just quaint fashion icons[25] but are—as the images tie lumberjacks to the Triangle Shirtwaist Fire, to mining, to the lynching and murder of IWW members in Centralia, Washington—part of a larger historical narrative about working people and their struggles. Implicitly, *Rough Crossing* argues that this particular history remains relevant. Like Tarale and Eleshia's project, *Rough Crossing* tries to move a public dialogue toward, at minimum, more respectful understanding of working-class experience.

Rough Crossing also negotiates many of the same boundaries that Tarale and Eleshia's project does. In the context of the course, it develops these students' sense of agency: they can find working-class writers I didn't include in the syllabus (and, apparently, should have, as their emphatic reflections about Anise indicate)—again, that Freirean sense of teacher-students and student-teachers. And, like their classmates, they were also bringing academic work off campus. In the most obvious way, the socially networked Tumblr enables this, allowing viewers to connect along areas of interest (the site linked to other Tumblrs that focus on working-class struggle) as well as with friends from school or work. The real-world promotion, strongly encouraged by me, links this virtual network to the nonvirtual world, allowing for connection beyond one's preconstructed online social network. It is publicly archived, available, and, as their web stats indicate, still being discovered by readers. This is everyday politics.

A website cannot have the types of conversations that often directly change hearts or minds, but it operates more like the poems in newspapers and photographs on walls discussed in the previous chapters, voicing the positions of absent interlocutors.[26] And, as with those poems and photos, the aesthetic richness of these texts—inventive, cross-genre, multimodal—reaches out differently and, thus, reaches different audiences (or the same conversants in different ways). This diversity of approaches is important in building coalitions around shared ideas. It's also important in creating a range of pathways to a more just world. These projects clearly make explicit claims for recognition: simply announcing that the working class exists and cannot be ignored is, in the United States today, no small feat. But they also engage in representation—literally bringing questions of class and class consciousness into a range of public conversations—and redistribution. *Rough Crossing*, on various pages, makes redistributionist claims (for public libraries, for worker safety), but it also explicitly engages in the redistribution of knowledge, bringing working-class experience and history out of archives and making them available to anyone who landed on the website.[27]

As for the organizers in Michigan and Tennessee, as for the anonymous recirculators after September 11, for Tarale and Eleshia and for Addison, Lindsay, and Sheree, texts became tactics. They used literature to engage in acts of recognition, representation, and redistribution. To do this, they made various campus-community connections that are captured, for many in higher education today, under the heading of "civic engagement." The similarities are there, it's true. But in the next section I will emphasize how their work is distinct from the best known of engagement practices: service learning.

Tactics vs. Service

Much of what I've discussed here—participatory research, linking campus with the wider world, even evoking "politics" at all, really—is tantamount for many faculty members (and, perhaps, even more administrators) to service learning. In 2012, Campus Compact estimated that 95 percent of institutions of higher education offer some service learning and, more remarkably, that nearly 50 percent of college students have engaged in service learning activities.[28]

But the projects I've discussed were not service learning. Despite some shared ambitions (and the well-developed institutional support structures service learning can unlock), I chose not to make American Working Class Literature a service learning course.[29] I did not want to be responsible for "forced volunteerism,"[30] with students providing "direct service . . . such as serving food at shelters, tutoring, blood drives, house renovations, or gardening."[31] I agree, to put it simply, with many of the well-known critiques of service learning. I'm concerned about its ties to *noblesse oblige* and about the idea that privileged students need to learn from their encounters with less privileged community members; I'm concerned about reifying class distinctions[32] and with taxing, rather than helping, the community organizations where my students volunteer.[33] But most importantly, I worry about service learning's ultimate relation to everyday politics; that it is, in Harry Boyte's telling metaphor, "a potential bridge to politics, but not politics."[34] I didn't want my students on a bridge—and a "potential bridge" seems awfully perilous. I wanted them, as much as possible, to be engaging in everyday politics, not acts of service that would in some ineffable way maybe make them more politically engaged at some indeterminate future point.

These objections are not new. And critics like those I've just been citing have developed many alternative, and more explicitly politicized, versions of service learning. Their approaches are diverse, and my intention here is not to survey them. Rather, I'll follow Tania D. Mitchell's superlative 2008 lit-review of the ranging field of (to use Mitchell's preferred term) "critical service-learning." These approaches differ from traditional service learning, according to Mitchell, primarily because of their "explicit aim toward social justice"—one of the clearest ways her work aligns with "next generation" civic engagement ideas, as I'll discuss more in the next chapter. Beyond that, she identifies two major practical differences: they focus on "developing authentic relationships" to the communities they engage; and they work "to redistribute power" in more equitable ways.[35] In this framework, you can't just show up and do service; you need to develop an understanding of the particular and unique features of the social problems that affect the population you are studying and attempt to solve them in more persistent ways than serving a plate of food or cleaning up trash one Sunday. The focus is structural, and the work is based not just on revolutionary creeds or high ideals but on thoughtful, persistent engagement with the problems you want to solve and the people they affect.

In American Working Class Literature we certainly pursued this "authentic" understanding. For Mitchell, that term includes striving for "reciprocity and interdependence," "shared understanding," "mutuality, respect, and trust."[36] In our class, we attempt to develop complex understandings and respect for the experience of class oppression. We study a range of figures, historical and contemporary, around the United States and across its borders. We discuss how characters feel—and how the mediating lens of the text helps (and sometimes limits) our understanding. We try to dig deep into the realities of working-class experience.

Some readers will, no doubt, be thinking that texts can't engage in "reciprocity" or "mutuality." It's true. There are limits to literature's work as a mediator.[37] But this limit isn't absolute and certainly shouldn't lead to outright dismissal. I know more about life in Africa than I otherwise would because of the African novels I've read. And some of my more privileged students, no doubt, experience our readings the way I experience Nigerian novels like *The Rape of Shavi* (1983) or *Americanah* (2013). This is, again, that familiar connection between reading literature and recognition. I *could* know much more about Africa, of course, just as many of my students could know more about working-class life. We could always recognize others better. But in a world with ever more and ever higher fences—whether between continents or communities—the fact that understanding is limited doesn't make it bad, just limited.[38]

And, as Mitchell notes, classroom discussion help buttress mediated understanding.[39] The course includes rich students and poor students (only some of whom identify as working class). By its nature, the class allows students to become—sometimes indirectly, sometimes because of direct commentary by their peers—aware of their privilege (or their lack of privilege) in new ways. This real diversity is one of the joys (and challenges) of teaching at a community college. And these conversations—more reciprocal, more mutual—complicate and enrich the experiences we've read about.

All of that, to me, feels like a version of authenticity. But if my course has its limits,[40] many service learning placements face even more barriers. As Mitchell notes, "Authenticity is not achieved in a semester, so an ongoing partnership and prolonged engagement in service are integral to achieving this desired outcome."[41] Serving someone food, hoeing in a garden for a few afternoons—this is, I'd argue, unlikely to produce any more authentic understandings than what I've just described. So while the class content and discussions push toward developing authentic understanding, the final project leans toward political action with a social justice orientation, the second of Mitchell's descriptors for critical service learning. While we assess the experiences of inequality and oppression, we're also studying solutions, most obviously, the literary responses that make up the course content, but also the things characters do in those texts: go on strike, become Communists, run away from oppressive conditions, kill their oppressors. We talk daily about the role of literature in this struggle—why authors write what they write, how they see it fitting into the struggle, and whether or not their version (or any version) might succeed at redressing such conditions.

The students' final projects, then, aren't just tacked on to the course as some kind of temporary, forced connection. Their projects are shaped by their developing understanding of the experience of class oppression and responses to it, both on and off the page. This link between course content and final project both reinforces authentic understanding and ties the students' work into my larger discussion in this book, where structural change is grounded in everyday politics but can still lead to transformations in civil society and law. The projects, then, not only attempt—"attempt" because just like final papers in more traditional classes, they don't all succeed—structural transformation, but try to achieve it based on authentic understandings of working-class experiences.

At this point, it may sound as if my course is totally aligned with the critical service-learning paradigm. But my students' work is not critical service learning, either. The problem for me with any service-based approach is the paradoxical disempowerment students experience with respect to their community organization. It's hard to do authentic work when you're just putting in your hours and doing what you are told. Strong collaboration between faculty and the partner organization, when it happens, can alleviate some of these concerns.[42] Even still, students will inevitably be limited, by the duration of their service, by presumptions (right or wrong) about their abilities, by the community partners' specific missions or their capacity to engage with the students' ideas. It's no surprise that a handful of studies indicate a preference, on the behalf of community organizations, for "transactional" relationships—slotting students into existing projects.[43] Service learners just don't have much power within community organizations.

This explicit hierarchy limits both potential learning and political potential. Yes, students may see and interact with people who are different from them (which is good); they may learn about how off-campus institutions work (also good). But they become a cog in an already existing system, part of someone else's strategy for change. They experience substantial limits on their chance to develop key political skills and to engage in the tactical interventions of everyday politics—which demands something more like equitable exchange, not a volunteer coordinator telling you what to do, not you "serving" someone.

This is my foundational concern with service learning. And it's emphasized by the findings of the Political Engagement Project, a sprawling Carnegie Institute research program that analyzed twenty-one courses at a wide range of colleges and universities with the goal of assessing how college helps to develop the broadly defined set of practices they term "responsible political engagement."[44] While most college educations touch on learning *about* politics (e.g., political history, political philosophy), few have adequately helped students "develop political goals and make informed decisions to advance them."[45]

The Political Engagement Project wants colleges to teach political action, which consists, in their lexicon, of four essential skills:

- Skills of political influence and action: such as knowing whom to contact to get something done about a social or political problem and persuading others to support one's political position

- Skills of political analysis and judgment: including the ability to write well about political topics and the ability to weigh the pros and cons of different political positions
- Skills of communication and leadership: for example, assuming leadership of a group and making a statement at a public meeting
- Skills of teamwork and collaboration: such as helping a diverse group work together and dealing with conflict when it arises[46]

The Political Engagement Project (PEP) was, of course, quite aware of how service learning might support these outcomes, and not only because Thomas Ehrlich was one of the lead investigators.

It's true, many service-learning placements clearly help students develop a sense of institutional power—"whom to contact to get something done about a social or political problem"—and would likely emphasize teamwork and collaboration (though more often than not, only with the other students who share their placement). But political analysis? Leadership? Students in traditional service placements, as I've just noted, can be somewhat sheltered from those experiences, precisely because these skills are difficult to develop and many students lack them. It's a circular problem for any service-learning placement.

Teaching students to use texts as tactics, I want to argue, focuses specifically on those essential skills—"analysis and action" as well as "leadership and judgment." Not surprisingly, these are, according to PEP, both more difficult to teach and more foundational to students' political development: "interventions with a strong emphasis on teaching political action skills are likely to have greater effects on students' internal political efficacy."[47] Developing these skills, to put it more simply, empowers students. In the short term, they become more like fellow activists or "colleagues" (a term preferred by some "next-generation" engagement scholars);[48] in the long term, practices of analysis and action can become foundational to their political commitments. In the work of my student-activists, I see both short- and long-term political developments in three key ways.

First, and most obviously, teaching students to use texts as tactics pushes for an intervention shaped by their unique understanding.

There's not really a predetermined menu of options. (Remember the ranging list of possibilities in my assignment and, as I mentioned, how students ignore them?) As we read and discuss, my students respond to the problems they identify through *interventions of their own creation.* Eric Sheffield forcefully argues for this shift in service learning: "Project choice must come out of student experience, for it is only there that genuine reflection can develop. Further reflection comes as student plans are formulated and put to the test in the problematic situation in order to evaluate their practical worth."[49] Students using texts as tactics necessarily invent their own modes of political engagement. They work as tacticians, their work "determined by the absence of a proper locus."[50] In encouraging this, rather than focusing on placement with a community organization, I strongly privilege authenticity of action: self-created, more closely aligned with our course's literary content, these projects offer more powerful learning opportunities.

So of course the students end up producing projects I couldn't have imagined. And that's the second major benefit: the space for *creative* intervention. As they think about target audiences (elected officials? their fellow students?), they consider how best to connect with and influence that audience's thinking. Their main goal—"persuading others to support [their] political position," in PEP's language—often becomes a creative question. Should they, for instance, approach the audience with a tone of challenge (like Amiri Baraka) or a more neutral tone (like Steinbeck)? Verse or prose or a mixture of the two—or, like Tarale and Eleshia, sociological sampling? Such options offer students not just rhetorical choices but, in making the decisions, useful leadership skills.

My students' tendency toward a creative sensibility surprised me at first. Yet having approvingly evoked Iris Marion Young throughout this book, I shouldn't have been surprised. Young argues, as I noted earlier, we need more ways to engage with others than simply rational debate and conversation.[51] The diverse modes of thought and of expression in creative projects echo—and reinforce the value of—this claim. The two examples I've covered here include fairly rational political survey questions about wages and union memberships but also more open questions about literature and class consciousness; *Rough Crossing*, with its stylized mixed media, is even more aesthetically textured. None of the students' projects—interviews, videos, zines, readings, music (from metal to freak folk)—cleave to traditional academic expectations like a term paper; this opens the projects to a greater diversity of audiences and helps students develop practices they can use elsewhere and to other ends. And, *after* seeing these projects, I really understood the longstanding tension between service learning and literature courses.[52] What community organization, I asked myself, could possibly support this work anyway? Would anyone let Tarale and Eleshia design the research project they were interested in—or be able to identify a use for it? What about Addison, Sheree, and Lindsay's website?[53] Few community organizations have the literary chops to support these approaches.[54] As students' projects innovate aesthetically, they illuminate just how real and troubling these boundaries are in our existing political and community structures.

The students' final projects exhibit, then, their "leadership and judgment" as well as their skills of "action and analysis" (that's PEP language again). But behind all this, in the shadow of the final projects, is a third, perhaps more important, feature: process skills. For instance, when the *Rough Crossing* group wanted to promote their site on the television screens positioned around our campus—which typically flash weather reports or key deadlines for financial aid—they had to figure out whom to talk to, what file type their poster had to be in. To take another example, when Sheree's requests for a number of interlibrary loan items were rejected, she pursued the ILL librarian (whose e-mail on our campus is deliberately anonymous), set up a meeting, and managed to get her hands on Special Collections books from another state![55] While not explicitly political, such work develops political skills of the first order. To change institutions, you have to know how they function. The students dealt with the powers of street-level bureaucracy (and, quite often, won).[56]

To call this "action and analysis" or "leadership" might sound boosterish, but everyday politics is, as I've emphasized throughout, not all speeches and rallies. Indeed, what is everyday politics if not, as in Tarale and Eleshia's project, conversations with strangers? Or collaboration with people who, while fellow students, are also quite different from you?[57] These projects evoke the skills of everyday politics at its most mundane: phone banking, door knocking, data entry. Mundane, yes, but you don't change the law—or even how people talk about the law—without knowing how to publicize your message.[58]

Getting outside the framework of service learning, then, puts students in a position to develop political skills. In using texts as tactics, they struggled with the everyday challenges familiar in most every political movement: leadership, creative problem solving, process. They didn't volunteer; they learned to practice—indeed, they *practiced*, as their final projects evidence, everyday politics.

I've been making two arguments here. One, particularly for people who think a lot about service learning, is that teaching texts as tactics more wholly develops the political skills advocated for by the Political Engagement Project than most service learning opportunities. It leads to increased—and increasingly effective—public engagement because it foregrounds students' analyses of the subject matter (literature and class, in this case) to build more authentic understandings than volunteerism can; and then it enables an explicit, practical link between those new understandings and the students' political action. Because students don't have community partners to tell them what to do or whom to talk to or (as is sometimes the case) to shield them from difficult situations,[59] they work to solve political problems on their own, tactically responding to the shifting terrain "in an infinite variety of ways."[60] Using texts as tactics as a mode of pedagogy serves as more than a bridge to politics: it teaches students about politics at all levels, while engaging them in the difficult work of everyday politics.

The distinction between tactics and service is more than just nomenclature; it's an epistemological shift. And it runs parallel to other moves in the world of "civic engagement" on campus; this is, as I'll discuss in the next chapter, an example of the politicized, activist work that "next-generation" public engagement practitioners seem to aspire to. This shift moves students (and instructors) from a model of volunteerism to one of collaborative everyday politics, from service project to shared labor for a more just world. My students, even as students, are doing work that is in most ways indistinguishable from the work of the readers who used texts as tactics in the earlier chapters here. And their successes—even if measured—offer some proof of that; they are doing more than simply studenting, volunteering, or serving. Using texts as tactics teaches them skills for engagement and for effective political action that they can use as students; but it is also leading to immediate acts of recognition, representation, and the redistribution of all-too-often siloed historical knowledge. Their work impacts them—as students, as humans—but also impacts all of us. And it enables future transformations.

That flash forward (even if I'm just speculating) encapsulates this chapter's second, bigger argument. What makes teaching texts as tactics an effective pedagogy is the same thing that makes it an effectual politics. As these interventions radiate outward in unpredictable ways—from the classroom into the community, from student work to the work of a lifetime—they can continue to change our world in ways we might not be able to imagine.

4

Reconnecting the Political

tactics, literary studies, and publicly engaged scholarship

So that's how people use texts as tactics. The first three chapters of this book tell very different stories of tactical reading: the mass publication of poems—in newspapers, on TV, on websites, and in public spaces—after September 11; the public reading and discussion of Steinbeck's *Grapes of Wrath* by two cities trying to sustain themselves during the Great Recession; the public conversations and web publication by my students, who used literature to open questions about class in America today.

That they are so different is important. It's a feature of the tactical: local, in-the-moment, created in response "to circumstances in an infinite variety of ways," a "use" that runs contrary to presumptive, or programmatic, uses.[1] These interventions are (even when supported by huge institutions like the National Endowment for the Arts) creative, grassroots, unexpected. Because they are not beholden to familiar instruments of politics—in particular, the US electoral system and its parties—they are more empowering to the tacticians and, as a function of that empowerment, richer with transformative potential. Still, despite these differences, three key features encouraged me to bring these particular examples together. They all show literature in mass public uses. This type of use is in itself somewhat unexpected in an era when literature's ongoing "death" shows up in headlines of major newspapers (and is accepted as a *fait accompli* by plenty of scholars who believe there is nothing outside the text anyway).[2] Despite all that, I've managed to find plenty of examples of literature in use not just by small publics—say, underground literary societies or college classrooms—but by large, diverse cross sections of people in the United States.[3]

To see this, I had to adjust my ideas about reading. I had to accept that not everyone reads like English majors—or their professors. Instead of looking for finely calibrated close readings or New Historical anecdotes, I looked for *all* the evidence of reading I could find: what people read, yes, but really what they said about reading, the ways ideas or themes from texts showed up in their lives and conversations, even just the way texts kept showing up in different places. In mass public use—and I think *only* in mass public use—literature can play a role in everyday politics.

That focus on mass public use provides, then, the foundation for all the claims I'm making in this book. The second feature shared by all these tactical reading practices is how their reading brings people together, not just people we know, but people we mostly pass on the street without a word (if we're even in the same part of town). As literary texts create these links—offering shared language, shared stories, shared practices—people can begin, in real-world situations, to work around and within difference, to connect with others and collaborate on issues of shared concern. Such connection is visible in the growing networks of collaboration in Jackson and Knoxville, in the re-publication cycles after September 11, and in the way my students collaborated with people (both in class and off campus) who were different from them.

The particular way using texts as tactics brings people together is clear in the distinction between "community" in its Big Read sense and "community" as a register of one's responsibility to others—a key point in the second chapter. The first community demands a kind of tribal pledge, even if it's unspoken; the second empowers people to collaborate without becoming the same. Public reading can function as intermediary, without common ethnic identity, without requiring adherence to a particular cultural lineage. And while some might want to suggest that reading canonical literature is a version of such cultural orthodoxy (that's true, in a very general sense), I would again point to the ways tactical readers respond to texts: not frozen in awe of Steinbeck's canonical status, but with equal measures of love and critique; willing to remix the canon to their own ends; asking strangers how *they* understand working-class literature, not telling them what it is. Tactical readers make of literature what they will and, in doing so, they open up the literary world's (sometimes exclusive) borders.[4]

Tactical readers work in public and they bring people together. On their own, these are noteworthy events. But these two features are, of course, coproductive: the more public you get, the more capacity you have to bring people together. But what really makes the reading practices I've been discussing important—their third shared feature—is how they help: delivering cans of food, offering advice about avoiding foreclosure, starting (or augmenting) a community group working to change policies around public housing. That's redistributive politics in its traditional sense. These readers also engaged in more unexpected political work: reclaiming rights denied, using those rights to argue for the recognition of others who might be in need, engaging in acts of representation (for people in poverty, for people victimized by racist assumptions). This is, as I've been arguing all along with Nancy Fraser's help, the work of justice.[5] And that's the second point: reading texts as tactics (to tweak a famous phrase from Auden—though not the Auden of "September 1, 1939"[6]) makes something happen. It reshapes our shared world.

So these readers work tactically in mass public settings; they use texts to bring people together, and they make something happen. This book's main work has been documenting stories that helped me build that definition. And, of course, the readers I've discussed to this point hardly provide the limit case. Many more readers have used texts as tactics, both in the period this book covers and throughout history.[7]

This book is a document of these remarkable practices. But another part of its work is translating the successes of these tactical readers, most of whom don't spend much of their time on college campuses, for more academic audiences. I began that task in the previous chapter and I complete it here—first, by placing tactical readers in conversation with two divergent academic discourses: literary studies, my disciplinary home, and the increasingly vast field of public engagement.

Both, I'll show, struggle around questions of politics, though in inverse ways: while literary studies is only too glad to claim great political impact (with little demonstrated result), many public engagement scholars have begun to lament the field's lack of political impact. Neither assessment, I would suggest, is quite accurate.

In the second section, I detail the framework—useful on both sides of this divide—that has helped me identify how readers, using texts as tactics, engage in acts of recognition, representation, and redistribution: how they, put more simply, do politics. That framework, a slightly modified version of Jürgen Habermas's theory of communicative action and deliberative democracy, helped me see how political change is characterized by multiple levels of intervention. Habermas provides a way to clearly see the link between microinteractions (like reading and conversations) and systemic political change.

Linking language and political practice, as Habermas does, offers a theoretical framing for the work of the tactical readers whom this book has spent so many words describing and analyzing. It also illuminates the existing political impact of a range of public engagement practices. So by bringing the tactical readers' theory of practice into a more explicitly theoretical context, I hope to open lines of communication between these multiple publics—the tactical readers I've written about here and the academy; the divergent fields of literary studies and public engagement. If we could better communicate, the possibilities for broader political transformation would only grow.

Missing Politics: Literary Criticism and Civic Engagement

I wrote this book because I was interested in how people could use literature in the practice of politics. But I started down that path because I found myself flabbergasted by literary critics who made truly outlandish claims about the political impact of a poem or a novel but based them on little more than their tortuous interpretation of its finest details.[8] To do what I wanted to do—to find people practicing politics with literature—I had to avoid the move that led to those grandiose claims, the keystone, acknowledged or not, of most literary criticism for a very long time: I couldn't close read.

While close reading has been defamed by many impressive scholars, particularly in its association with the New Criticism's retrograde politics,[9] it remains omnipresent. Even when we don't call it "close reading." The move of attending to a text's nuances and quirks in hyperconscious detail maintains, as Eric Hayot recently put it, a "nearly theological" appeal for all sorts of critics. Hayot has picked a good metaphor. Theologically speaking, close reading transcends denomination:

> a deconstructive reading of a text or paratext connects its reader to large-scale mysteries of language or being, and a New Historicist reading of an anecdote or private letter manages, from its humble origins, to adumbrate the essential premises of an entire era.[10]

Close reading is everywhere.[11]

I haven't avoided close readings because I don't like them or don't enjoy doing them.[12] My concern is that what someone with a highly specialized, to say nothing of culturally and economically stratified, training sees in a text is probably not what most people see. Hayot's religious metaphor is most apt in this sense: theological devotees are often cloistered, and being cloistered disconnects you, definitionally, from others. Which, again, is fine if you want to be alone with people who are, more or less, just like you. But if you want to see literature playing a part in everyday politics—outside the sect of the seminar room or the MLA convention—it's not an effective approach.

The path out of close reading, for many politically inclined literary scholars in the last century, has been sociology.[13] And sociology is, once again, ascendant in literary studies; as James English recently noted, a "wide . . . swath of the discipline has undergone some form of sociological reorientation" since the 1980s.[14] Given my political commitments and my ambition to escape close reading, it shouldn't be much of a surprise that this "new" sociology of literature provides part of the background for this book.[15] But while I was fishing in the Frankfurt School, while I was digging into archives with Robert Darnton and Roger Chartier[16] and mapping with Pascale Casanova and Franco Moretti, I was avoiding (mostly because of my ignorance) the more obvious link between academic work and everyday politics: the field of civic engagement. From community service to service learning, from anchor institutions to institutional partnerships, community engagement since the mid-1980s has steadily increased in volume and capacity on most college campuses; this growth has, according to many accounts, "reinvigorated and advanced the democratic purposes of higher education."[17]

How did I miss all of that? Short answer: I did my graduate work in English departments. As Linda Flower puts it, a scholar working in "a public space" marks "the greatest break with the modern discipline of English": a discipline defined, in large part, by the fairly *private* practice of close reading.[18] Thus, it's no surprise that as engagement gained currency across campus, literary studies hesitated.[19] The tension is temperamental as well as practical: the discipline's "hermeneutics of skepticism" collide awkwardly with the "explicit hopefulness" that characterizes much public scholarship.[20] All of which is to say that my resistance was, at least in part, acculturated—hardly, as other younger scholars have noted, an unusual experience for someone who was a graduate student in the first decade of the twenty-first century.[21] But even as I got over that and recognized some kindred spirits in the field, I hesitated because of what I saw as the political limits of this ostensibly political approach.

There's a hierarchy problem built in to "service," as I argued in the previous chapter. Similarly, the most common adjective attached to "engagement"—at least until recently—has been "civic," a word that certainly has its own baggage. "Civic," at its root, presumes citizenship and a commitment to the governmental order; "civic" engagement, then, disenfranchises the millions of people who make their homes where their citizenship is met with hostility, both in a legal sense (viz. unending battles over citizenship and immigration) and as a social practice (as for the racially profiled people I discussed in the first chapter). "Civic" action alone won't fix an oppressive system.

Even if you want to dismiss my concerns as mostly semantic (or backward looking, or too focused on a revolution that is, at best, a long way off), the field is also marked by specific instances of its own political quietude.[22] As "civic scholars" have built programs and partnerships, they have avoided important fights: failing, as John Saltmarsh and Matt Hartley have recently acknowledged, to support ethnic studies and other departments when they were under fire—or simply investing in overly capitalistic visions of "community development."[23] Critics could also point out, as Talmage A. Stanley (among others) has, that civic engagement just hasn't done enough:

> hundreds of communities, among them the same places in which students are engaged and with which the college has partnership agreements, face a loss of vitality and increasingly limited options for sustainable development, their civic life diminished and lessened.[24]

Despite the effort, public engagement has "not been able to help shape the regional or national debate on the accessibility of rural healthcare."[25]

To be clear, these are not critiques lobbed from the sidelines. Stanley runs the successful Appalachian Center for Civic Life at Emory & Henry College; two of those quotes above are from John Saltmarsh, a foundational figure in the field.

So what's engagement missing? It turns out my hesitations around its politics were not so far off the mark. According to Saltmarsh, Hartley, and Clayton, "What has emerged is a remarkably *apolitical* 'civic' engagement."[26] Abby Kiesa puts it even more precisely: The "narrow definition" of engagement visible "at conferences, trainings, and in research" leaves out "political engagement (electoral, policy- and issue-focused, and otherwise)."[27] The Political Engagement Project, whose work I quoted extensively in the last chapter, makes a similar point about how "American higher education pays relatively little attention to undergraduate students' political learning."[28]

One might suggest civic engagement has bought its home in the academy with its promise of an apolitical approach to problems that demand political solutions. Or, as Saltmarsh and Hartley put it, "the civic engagement movement realized greater acceptance through an emphasis on depoliticized pedagogy, curriculum, and student learning."[29] In a slightly more generous frame, one might suggest that civic engagement is founded on an intellectual error in which "partisan activities and political awareness and agency are being confounded."[30] Apolitical on purpose or by accident—both are disappointing considerations. And, whatever the cause, the result is clear: "students lose opportunities to learn about the influence of the political system on issues and communities . . . and miss alternative models of politics."[31] Indeed, something quite similar might be said of faculty as well. If we want political impact, we are stuck making claims in arcane journals about (in my discipline) the revolutionary nature of obscure poems. We operate in systems that hold great political potential; but without connections to everyday politics, we're *all* on what Harry Boyte (in a quote I used in the previous chapter) criticized as "a potential bridge to politics."[32] We're thinking politics, but we're not actually accomplishing much of anything.

That's a quick sketch of some of the political limits of literary criticism *and* the some of the political limits of public engagement scholarship. Positioning myself here between the grandiose claims of politics in my home discipline and the limited politics of public engagement, one thing seems clear: neither is political enough.

Politics is about creating power "for people with diverse interests and views to build the common world" and instantiating that power in legal protections;[33] it's about, in the terms I've used throughout, achieving justice through acts of recognition, representation, and redistribution. In that light, both fields could use a better way to understand not just *how to* create the power that can be used to make the world more just—but *how to understand* the way the things we already do might (and might not be) part of achieving those ends.

My answer to the first question is spelled out across the first three chapters: the public, tactical practices that bring people together and actuate material redistribution, political representation, or social recognition. That work, carried out here by tactical readers, provides a grounding for politics in literary studies *and* offers some ideas for the "next-generation" engagement scholars I've been quoting, like Stanley, Longo, Kiesa, and Saltmarsh. Through a focus on tactical collaboration, scholars can use our existing knowledge and skills—in teaching and facilitation, in research, in grant writing or poetry writing—to participate in a more widely impactful practice of politics. With a few tweaks, such as taking reading and making it public or taking interpretation of texts and making them shared, our professional practices can do more.

But skeptical readers will no doubt wonder what precisely these things achieve. For some, the previous three chapters will not be enough to back up these claims. For them, I want to turn to the second question: clarifying how to understand what work is political, how to recognize the political impacts we are making.

Kevin Bott, of Imagining America, recently offered a simple answer to that question: to "solve real-world issues that threaten the great democratic experiment" of the United States, it is necessary to "frame [scholarly] work within a broader theory of change related to the revival of robust participatory democracy at large."[34] Bott is speaking of a need in public engagement; but such a theory is, not surprisingly, also missing from literary studies. I agree with Bott: such a theory would help scholars in public engagement and in literary studies. With the right theory, scholars in both fields could recognize the ways they are already doing politics and—deploying some of the tactical approaches I've described throughout this book —identify clearer paths toward greater impacts.

In the next section, I'll describe how Jürgen Habermas's theory of communicative action and deliberative democracy offers that frame; and I will account for its mysterious absence from these discussions. Habermas's theory situates politics against a large horizon while remaining sensitive to how everything from conversations to newspapers to libraries to social service agencies—not just rallies and legislation —can have significant impacts. He acknowledges the rapacious power of systems like capitalism but without teleological assumptions of revolution. In short, he offers a compelling way to understand how politics happens: from the most basic encounter between a reader and a text to large-scale structural changes. As such, he can help us reconnect politics in both fields.

Engaging Politics with Habermas

This section offers an overview of Habermas's theory of communicative action and deliberative democracy. This theory is Habermas's major philosophical contribution, though you wouldn't know it from how he's cited: according to Google Scholar, his *Structural Transformation of the Public Sphere* (1962) garners almost six times as many mentions as the work I'm discussing here. I've argued elsewhere that this under-reading of Habermas is a loss, as his mature philosophy corrects some of the shortsighted flaws in his early work and offers a way of attending to how politics happens through language (in its many manifestations), public spheres, civil society, and, ultimately, laws.[35] More importantly, it offers some compelling ways to link these levels of social practice. As such, it helps explain my sense of how many public practices (for obvious reasons, I focus on the reading and discussion of literature) can be recognized as part of politics.

In what follows, I'll situate Habermas's work briefly in intellectual history, particularly with respect to the "first generation" of the Frankfurt School. Then I'll illustrate the main premises of his theory of communicative action and deliberative democracy with examples from the previous chapters. I'll show *how* his theory helps scholars interested in public engagement recognize our current political impacts—and how we can achieve greater impacts.

Born in Germany in 1929, Habermas came of age in the midst of global catastrophe, and his intellectual formation was steeped in the cynicism of the postwar European intelligentsia, a cynicism exemplified, perhaps, by his mentors Horkheimer and Adorno. Even early in his career, however, Habermas was at odds with this consensus. He disagreed with Adorno about the revolutionary potential of art; he studied structures and systems of political power that other members of the Frankfurt School dismissed; he expressed skepticism about Marxist teleology. At least in part because he wouldn't take a room at the Grand Hotel Abyss, he left Frankfurt as a graduate student.[36] Yet Habermas is rooted in the critical theory of the Frankfurt School: so much so that a decade after his departure, he would return to take Horkheimer's chair in philosophy and later would serve (twice) as director of the Institute for Social Research. Habermas's biographical link to Frankfurt is clear enough; and, closely examined, his intellectual connection is as well—particularly if one goes back to the school's foundational ambitions.

In 1931, Horkheimer, taking over leadership of the Institute, defined its task as developing "the kind of theory which is an element in *ac-*

tion leading to new social forms [and] is not a cog in an already existent mechanism."[37] Horkheimer here was already developing the argument most familiar from *Dialectic of Enlightenment* (1947) that "traditional theory," in its adherence to rationalized, capitalist logics, could only support modern society's oppressive tendencies—thus Horkheimer's proposition of a "theory which projects . . . a solution to the distress" and "does not labor in the service of an existing reality." This call to praxis repeats again and again, as Horkheimer evokes a theory that is "not something self-sufficient and separable from the struggle," but a part of the work of producing a more equitable, more human world.[38] Critical theory, then, is essentially a theory of practice.

Whatever their other disagreements, Habermas shares this fundamental ambition with Horkheimer. His language is rarely as bracing as Horkheimer's; yet writing in the late 1970s, he would declare,

> The point is to protect areas of life that are functionally dependent on social integration through values, norms, and consensus formation, to preserve them from falling prey to the systemic imperatives of economic and administrative subsystems.[39]

Systems, in much of Habermas's theory, are the enemy; almost all are driven by the rise of capitalism, which marks "a deformation, a reification of the symbolic structures of the lifeworld under the imperatives of subsystems differentiated out via money and power and rendered self-sufficient."[40] At another point, he compares these systems to "colonial masters coming into a tribal society" to "force a process of assimilation upon it."[41]

The goal of his philosophy, then, is to understand how we might protect the ways of life people have created for themselves—and not just because lives and cultures are valuable (they are), but because such spaces are the foundations of resistance to oppressive systems. Places where people build what he calls "counterinstitutions" that can "set limits to the inner dynamics of the economic and political-administrative action systems."[42] Habermas's prose isn't destined to be spray-painted on walls or shouted during protests. Yet his theoretical work all turns on the fundamental ambition of radical transformation, albeit from a position tethered to the confines of our world. Put another way, Habermas maintains radical hope—one of his most obvious bridges to public-engagement scholars—but also pragmatic skepticism. This is a powerful tool but also an unfashionable one. Much as Habermas's hope puts him at odds with many Frankfurt School members, his practicality pits him against other thinkers of his generation on the left, many of whom are more commonly discussed in literary studies.

To put it very generally, Habermas stands against the theoretical style that, in Timothy Brennan's phrase, "declares itself as *immediately* political—whose theory is a politics performed."[43] One version of this focuses on questions of identity, "*the first of political problems*," as popular political theorists Ernesto Laclau and Chantal Mouffe argue; against this Habermas has tried to conceptualize a politics that can work across and among identities.[44] Michael Hardt and Antonio Negri have generated much attention by identifying a "new form of sovereignty" —transnational, vicious, attacking even our DNA—they call "Empire" and arguing that we must fight against its amorphous encroachment in amorphous ways.[45] While Hardt and Negri essentially dismiss the value of national politics (and nations themselves), Habermas resolutely focuses on nations and transnational governments (like the European Union), which unquestionably exert power on our everyday lives in myriad ways.[46]

Habermas may be dull, but just as he maneuvered past the Grand Hotel Abyss's self-affirming pessimism to maintain the power of Frankfurt School critical theory, he avoids fights over identity and the groundless optimism of the "anarchist sublime," where revolution is always already being enacted (as in Hardt and Negri's subsequent work *Multitude* [2004]).[47] His theory offers tools to engage everyday politics in the world today based, as he says, on "a skeptical evaluation of current world conditions."[48]

Situating Habermas's political ambitions in this broad sense serves, I hope, as a proffer of his bona fides. For scholars who are happy to cite Marx or Horkheimer or Adorno, Habermas should be part of the conversation as well. This is equally true if you like Dewey: American pragmatism is one of the ways Habermas leavens Frankfurt orthodoxy.

If you are interested in the revolutionary potential of education conceived by Freire or hooks or Giroux, Habermas enframes their pedagogy in a larger theory of political transformation. If a practical approach to making political change is what you want, Habermas can help.

Much in the way Marx begins *Capital* (1867) with capitalism's "elementary form," the commodity, Habermas's work begins with another elementary form: interpersonal conversation.[49] Not the arm-twisting of a salesperson or the rhetorical sleight of hand of a politician, not the kind of conversation aimed at "individual successes"—"communicative action," says Habermas, is conversation with the goal of "reaching understanding" and taking action on shared goals.[50] The previous chapters of this book have included plenty of examples of communicative action: people talking and working toward agreements on actions with broad benefits, including the conversations between the groups organizing Big Read events that would serve patrons of both the library and the YWCA in Knoxville; conversations (invisible to us) between poetic republishers about which poem to publish or how to excerpt it; conversations between two people who stopped to look at a poem tacked up to a telephone pole; conversations between two members of a reading group in Jackson or between my students and strangers on a train; and, in every case, of course, between readers and texts. These conversations are foundational not just for politics but for existence: "the human species maintains itself through . . . communication," as Habermas points out; communicative action is the "elementary form" of our survival.[51] Without it, we cannot continue to exist.

Habermas (again, relentlessly practical) acknowledges that this linguistic coordination is never easy; he's not a normative thinker. Inequality, based on race or gender, class or sexual orientation, education or national status, and language ability, entwines itself in every conversation.[52] Yet as the tactical readers in the previous chapters illustrate, it is possible to work within and around these identities: indeed, tactical readers used Steinbeck's novel to talk about immigration with their neighbors; readers used poems critical of nationalism to reach those who might not have heard such ideas; my students used working-class literature to strike up conversations with strangers with varied political (and literary) views.

Communicative action doesn't always lead to transformation; Habermas rejects teleology. But as in Marx's opening analysis of the commodity, the micro-unit provides the basis for understanding both systemic oppression and means of resistance. Building from the foundation of the conversational dyad, Habermas's theory of communicative action and deliberative democracy suggests four levels at which communication and coordination can lead to political transformation: lifeworlds, public spheres, civil society, and legal regulation. Again, not every conversation reaches all these levels. But some (as the previous chapters have shown) can. Some conversations move beyond their initial interlocutors and form a network. Readers in a book club talked about *The Grapes of Wrath*, then went home and talked about it with their families; a teacher read Auden's poem, photocopied it, and gave it to her colleagues; a web surfer visited the *Rough Crossing* Tumblr and reblogged it. Habermas, writing in the 1990s, might well be describing these practices: "a network of communicative actions that branch out through social space and historical time" and simultaneously "live off sources of cultural traditions and legitimate orders no less than they depend on the identities of socialized individuals."[53] Some networks are limited, of course, to one or two conversations, but many have quite broad impacts.

Think about, as one example, Jackson community organizer Jon Hart. He participated in planning conversations for the Big Read, talked to his book club about *Grapes*, was in church for Cynthia Landrum's two sermons based on the novel. That's a network, both spatial and temporal, of interactions enabled by the cultural resource of Steinbeck's novel. And having met Jon, I'd speculate he was also talking about the book with his wife (who was in Kate Lambert Lee's *Faces of Poverty* photos), his coworkers (like Jessie Murray, with whom he shares an office), his clients at the Community Action Agency, and his friends. After all, Steinbeck was, as he told me, his "favorite or second-favorite author."[54] Parts of Hart's conversations, no doubt, evoked things students in literature courses might say; others clearly would not.

Such talk links one network to others; ideas and language from one conversation develop and spread to other conversations. Percolating out, talk generates shared understandings, the background of any conversation, which Habermas names the "grammar of forms of life."[55] This environment—constantly produced in conversations; constantly revised in conversations—is what Habermas calls the lifeworld. Its constant reproduction saves it from the exclusive, static sense of "community," as I discussed in the second chapter. Talk, in a divided and polarized world, is one of the few tools we have to build bridges. And talk about literature seems to me a particularly good tool for developing such bridges. It allows readers to encounter new words, new narratives, new ideas—or new formulations of familiar notions. Literature is part of the "cultural traditions" that provide a baseline (made up of words, narratives, and ideas) to facilitate new conversations with friends and family or conversations with new interlocutors. Reading enriches and complicates the lifeworld. Someone in the United States reading Lorna Dee Cervantes's "Palestine" encounters the words of a Chicana poet quoting a Palestinian poet; someone reading *The Grapes of Wrath* in 2009 learns new ways of expressing the struggles of living in poverty. Some readers will appreciate Ma Joad's use of pathos and family to talk about poverty; some will appreciate her son's more fiery rhetoric; for some, seeing Lange's *Migrant Mother* image on *Rough Crossing* will be the key to a new understanding.

It's not quite the exalted terms we usually use to praise literature, but what I'm suggesting is that literature offers the grist for new shared understandings; and, as mass audiences encounter a text and engage it through conversation, these new ideas percolate through communicative networks. And these networks, based in literary language, are (as I've noted with the help of Iris Marion Young) more inclusive than a network based on purely rational discussion and debate.[56] So if enough conversations happen—the case in the stories I narrated in the previous chapters—ideas that have developed within the lifeworld can begin to impact public spheres.

Contrary to his earliest conception of "the public sphere" in the 1960s (the one that's been cited in nearly twenty thousand publications) Habermas's mature conception builds on Nancy Fraser's well-known critique that every public sphere is made up of "competing counterpublics."[57] Thus Habermas, writing in the 1990s, defines the public sphere less as a static space (a coffeehouse) and more as "a network for communicating information and points of view" to many hearers so that "the streams of communication are, in the process, filtered and synthesized in such a way that they coalesce into bundles of topically specified *public* opinions."[58] Bundled together—coalescing around language, rhetoric, ideas—conversations are amplified and, as such, can bring in multiple new speakers and listeners.

The public sphere, then, isn't a single place welcoming only a particular segment of the population but is made up of spaces, linked together in myriad ways. The previous chapters visited many such spaces: public transit and public schools, movie theaters and churches, transitional housing facilities and libraries. These more obviously public spaces are linked, in Habermas's thinking, to the "isolated readers, listeners, and viewers" connected by the publicity of poems reproduced in mass media flows, on the web, in discussions of *Grapes* on local access television.[59] The power of this less exclusive, less static conception of the public sphere is clear in its organizational potential:

> The one text of "the" public sphere, a text continually extrapolated and extending radially in all directions, is divided by internal boundaries into arbitrarily small texts for which everything else is context; *yet one can always build hermeneutical bridges from one text to the next.*[60]

Thus we might conceive of the public sphere as the various venues where various counterpublics, having built their messages with more limited communities, put forth their ideas in the hope of finding more adherents: Big Read organizers make their commitments public in the Services Fair; poetic republishers make their ideas public in streets and mass media; my students make their work public on the web and in conversations.

Tactical readers, as I've argued throughout, engage with texts and talk to others about them. As that sharing of ideas reaches more and more people, connections are formed in familiar networks, and "hermeneutical bridges" can be built with multiple publics. While I'm focused on tactical readers here, the point stands equally well for many of the best-known engagement practices: community-based research builds bridges, shared leadership of off-campus work builds bridges, even service learning, it seems to me, might be understood as a bridgehead (though probably not a complete bridge).[61]

These are first steps. Then, as this sharing of language and ideas reaches a critical mass, which, of course, doesn't always happen, it begins to shape not just hermeneutics, but social practices, ways of living. I think the previous chapters have shown how such work is both inclusive and transformative.

The negotiation of language, the sharing of ideas, the debate; the building of lifeworlds and public spheres from the basis of such conversations —all of this rhymes with Boyte's conception of everyday politics.[62] Boyte, whose phrase I've been borrowing since the first pages, values these levels of grassroots interaction far above what he calls "politics as usual": the highly mediated (and commoditized) performance of electoral politics in the United States. Habermas, too, has strongly critiqued the failures of electoral politics.[63] And like Boyte, he values these foundational levels. They support existing spaces and practices (and help develop new ones); the range of possibilities in this politics emphasizes, again, the value of tactical actions. These newly constructed or newly created spaces, of course, serve as the means by which greater resistance to such systems may be shaped.

But Habermas goes a step beyond Boyte—and beyond many of the practitioners of civic engagement—by emphasizing how everyday politics is often (though not necessarily) deeply linked to civil society and ultimately the law. Public spheres can exercise power beyond their confines: discussions "continually extrapolated and extending radially" can "*build hermeneutical bridges*" into the realm of civil society and, ultimately, government.[64] This means changing mass public opinions and making sure these opinions have the protection of law—not just recognition or even representation, but a new distribution of power based on these goods.

For Habermas, law is based in its protection of human rights and its guarantee of the political autonomy to (if necessary) make new laws as public opinion changes. He also emphasizes the necessary foundation of a law that supports "living conditions" that allow "equal opportunities to utilize [these] civil rights."[65] Laws can be oppressive but also can be used (and changed) as a means to empowerment.

Of course not all conversations shape the law. But this book has given examples of how, by using texts as tactics, readers communicated in ways that reached this level of political efficacy. Using poems, readers made calls for the legal equality, respect, and, indeed, survival that were threatened in the fall of 2001 and, by virtue of these calls, reclaimed rights of speech and used that speech to represent diverse publics in the political process. Tactical readers in Jackson also leveraged governmental power—most obviously in the form of federal funding—in very immediate ways: they fed those who needed a meal, helped find housing for those who were losing theirs. Faced with systems of power that were suppressing their rights to existence, even to human sustenance, these tactical readers were working at every level of Habermas's system. And while more mundane, it's important to note that their legal success is also reflected in the ways elected figures (Knoxville's mayor and Jackson's congressperson) used texts as tactics to connect with constituents. While I would agree with Boyte that the practices of everyday politics are more important than such performative politics, the symbolic value is hardly negligible. Elected officials gathering with constituents to discuss matters of shared concern—issues, like immigration and economic inequality, that few politicians are eager to discuss in any depth—marks another strength of tactical reading. Using texts as tactics, readers built networks of communication that had impacts beyond their own intimate circles, beyond the public spheres they most commonly inhabit.

From conversation to public spheres to civil society and the law—that is a quick (and sympathetic) glance at the architecture of Habermas's theory of communicative action and deliberative democracy. And I hope by placing examples of tactical readers within this system, I have made more sense of Habermas's fairly abstract theory. But having mixed in tactical readers, I need to admit that Habermas wouldn't agree with all my examples. Since the theory's first articulation in the early 1980s, he has resisted art's role in communicative action. Elsewhere I've argued that the distinction that leads him to ignore literature is not one entailed by his larger theory; in fact, I think it is mostly the product of philosophical disputes that have little bearing on the theory's practical application.[66]

That's a larger conversation. For now, let me suggest that whether or not Habermas would endorse my application, his theory's radical insight is useful for my particular argument here and speaks, quite directly, to the political anxieties in recent public engagement scholarship. The way he breaks down the practice of politics into four levels helps make sense of both systemic oppression and the revolutionary potential coordinated, at bottom, by language. In this way, Habermas unites micro and macro analysis, which might allow literary critics to recognize the way the use of books by readers can both be shaped by and reshape systems; this approach can simultaneously help public engagement scholars discover some of the ways they can see change happening as a result of their good works.

Not every conversation changes the world. But as Habermas theorizes—and as the work of these tactical readers suggests—language, particularly literary language taken up in everyday conversation, holds the power to do so.

Despite the sprawling complexity of Habermas's ideas, he grounds the work of politics in everyday practices that can help scholars avoid resorting to gratuitous claims of power or defaulting to laments about powerlessness. And his focus on language makes him particularly effective in clarifying the ways literature, used tactically, shapes conversations and ideas, builds networks, and begins to change the world. That, at least, has been my specific argument for literary critics.

These insights, as Habermas would be the first to say, have a resonance far afield of literature. As I've described his theory, I've been gesturing to the political powers of publicly engaged scholarship. Let me return to the examples of political "failure" from above to suggest how, seen in a Habermasian light, they are more politically accomplished than they appear—and how they are capable of doing more.

When Stanley sighs that his work has not "been able to help shape the regional or national debate" around rural healthcare, Habermas's theory suggests he may not be using the right metric for assessing political efficacy. It seems quite easy to see, in Stanley's case, that the Freirean co-learner/coeducator model used in more than a third of all classes at his college *is* having real impacts. It appears, in Habermasian language, to be operating at the level not just of conversation, but of building public spheres and linking them—through student work on campus, through partnership with civil society institutions off campus. These actors are not trapped in the limited sense of "community" I discussed in chapter 3; they are organizing across communities for change.

But massive changes like healthcare for all—or even, with recent US history as a guide, improved healthcare for some—take an awful lot of time. Stanley's emphasis on failing to achieve what he calls "second-order change" (mass impacts, new laws) mistakes second-order change for politics. It fails to acknowledge the political power of the acts of recognition, redistribution, and representation that are clearly part of the college's large and ongoing project. Could there be more advocacy work, communication with legislatures? Lobbying by faculty and students? Opening of public health clinics with the college's (or the government's) money? Certainly. Perhaps more focus on the Political Engagement Project's outcomes, which I discuss in chapter 3, could shape this dimension of the work. But the current work is not a failure of politics, it's *part* of those larger projects, part of building the "hermeneutical bridges" and new, unexpected practices within civil society that make subsequent legislation possible.

A similar anxiety is clear in Nicholas Longo, Abby Kiesa, and Richard Battistoni's chapter in *Publicly Engaged Scholars: Next-Generation Engagement and the Future of Higher Education* (2016); the book itself is a kind of manifesto for the changing field. The three authors (echoing Boyte) argue for new engagement practices that would be "not an alternative to politics, but rather an 'alternative politics.'"[67] At this level,

I'm with them. But to achieve those ends, they favor large-scale program building and structural commitments: "sustained, developmental programs, with both curricular and cocurricular components"; not "single-service/single-course student engagement experiences."[68] The emphasis on that wide horizon (big-picture, long-term) echoes, I think, Stanley's second-order focus. And, again, aiming at structural change is not a *bad* ambition. But it misses the ways that tactical interventions—a single course or part of a single course; a brief engagement project or community-based research that doesn't last for years—are part of, even foundational to, political change. Unfortunately, Longo and his coauthors argue explicitly against this approach in favor of a "less tactical, more visionary" strategy. [69]

For these engagement scholars, the macro focus is a key to political impact. But that focus skips over the very real political work of tactical engagement; and it ignores some of the very real risks that come with institution building. Let me briefly point to three of the risks of big picture, macro-focused strategy.

First, it necessarily militates against the simultaneous calls these authors make for more *democratic* public engagement. Longo, Kiesa, and Battistoni signify that ambition by titling their article "The Future of the Academy with *Students as Colleagues*" (my emphasis); Saltmarsh, Hartley, and Clayton go further, defining the new "democratic engagement" as focused on "inclusiveness, participation, task sharing, lay participation . . . and an equality of respect for the knowledge and experience that everyone contributes to education and community building."[70] This evocation of grassroots democratic practice is praiseworthy: it's part of what Bott, as quoted earlier in this chapter, calls for, part of what I see in the work I've described in the previous chapters. But larger, more sustained structures are rarely a means to more democratic engagement; more often, they serve as a check on grassroots democracy—as in problematic service learning arrangements where students have no voice in the tasks they are assigned; as in well-established organizations that have only pre-determined pathways for new participants to engage.

Balancing these exigencies of stronger community ties that lead to wider and more durable impacts versus empowering students or faculty may be possible. But simultaneously building more coherent institutional structures and treating students—and other faculty and community partners who will be subject to those structures—as colleagues doesn't seem like a plausible balance in today's academic context. It's very difficult to be more institutional *and* more grassroots at the same time. Other engagement scholars, like Dan Butin, have recently expressed similar concerns.[71]

On this point of democratic engagement, my concerns go deeper—to the roots of our institutions of higher education. Our degree-granting role necessarily militates against an internal capacity for democratic practices. No matter how valiantly engagement scholars fight for a more central role for engagement, engagement seems to me unlikely, for the vast majority of students, to be the main focus in their degree-pursuing lives of (ever-growing) debt and job expectations and family and uncertainty. I see this all too often at my chronically underfunded community college, where students literally apologize that they can't take American Working Class Literature because their financial aid will cover only the precise classes that get them to their degrees; where students ask what kind of job a course that focuses on social justice will get them. It's easy for faculty to forget these pressures—we've already got our degrees!—but the majority of the people in our institutions wouldn't be there if we couldn't offer them a degree. Thus, an inherent power imbalance exists: we have the degrees; students want them. And it's further exacerbated by the transitory nature of studentship. Large-scale political change takes time. Yet students' presence on a campus is temporally bound and is marked by increasing instances of transfer between institutions, absences of a term or a year.[72] Many will, under these conditions, have a hard time developing agency within yet another large, complex structure on campus (and one that is no doubt different from the structure they may have known at their previous institution).[73]

This transitory reality is true, also, of the new faculty majority: precarious laborers who work without the respect of tenure or even long-term job contracts.[74] As such, more faculty inevitably move between campuses—across their careers, throughout the week, and even daily. At best, these conditions challenge faculty members' ability to place themselves within large-scale, ongoing projects; at worst I fear these faculty struggle even to know whom to speak with about such work (or where to find the time to have the conversation).

As these examples show, our higher education system, mirroring the United States at large, is structured to make political engagement difficult. The time and agency necessary for people—students, faculty, community collaborators—to engage in politics is almost impossible to find. And these limits stretch from community colleges like mine to, as Abby Kiesa has shown, elite institutions where the financial and temporal support for such work is, at least in theory, greater.[75]

So I'm with Kiesa, Longo, and Battistoni, with Saltmarsh, with Stanley in their advocacy for a higher-education system that is more invested in change, more responsive to community needs, more empowering of everyone. I'm just afraid that world is a very long way off—both on campus and beyond.

For now, tactical intervention may be what is possible. That's why I've advocated, across this book, for tactics that need little more than a book club meeting, a quick trip to the copy machine, or a ticket to ride public transit. Tactics are adaptable to different terrain, different audiences, and a wide range of actors—from desk clerks to mayors; community organizers to retirees. And tactics work on campus as well, as I've argued in the last two chapters. We can't escape the institution, but tactics do give us novel approaches to work within and around its limits; as I've shown, some tactical approaches can sneak politics past existing constraints, make claims that slip around censors, create resistance in the small fragments of time we salvage from our days: important features, as we all live with unprecedented demands on our time and new threats to our academic freedom.[76] Tactical practices can also sail on the currents that gust so many people through higher education today: following students as they go to other campuses, to jobs, to movements; following faculty as they, too, move between campuses, between jobs, between movements.[77] Operating tactically on campus, we can link our teaching, service, and research to create new approaches to politics by empowering students, precarious faculty, or tenured and tenure-track faculty.

To put it less grandly, a focus on tactics is realistic about what kinds of political interventions are possible—certainly in English departments, with their resistance to public engagement and their confusion about what constitutes politics; and quite possibly in the field of engagement itself, which risks the continued sacrifice of political power as it pushes to build more institutional structures to support itself. And to focus on the plausible isn't, at least in this case, to concede power. Working tactically is working for justice in its many forms; as I've argued throughout, tactics are tools for actuating recognition, representation, and redistribution. Tactics are powerful—powerful *and* plausible—in our larger world and in the context of contemporary higher education. That, in a sentence, is why this book has focused on tactics. But this chapter has turned, with Habermas's help, to showing how we might understand those practices, small as they may seem, as parts of a much larger political project. We don't achieve justice *only* by changing laws; we must work to achieve it piecemeal, through everyday politics. Without such work, larger changes will always be far off.

By fostering the space to develop new, more inclusive, more inventive practices of politics, by linking new practitioners into our already existing projects in new ways, we scale toward that structural, "second-order" change. Working tactically, I hope to have shown, with Habermas's help, that greater transformation is possible. Tactical work is democratic, inclusive, and immediately impactful. It matters *now*, even as it forms the basis for larger interventions to come.

Epilogue

building a better world

Maybe it's as simple as photocopying some poems and sticking them up around your neighborhood or passing them out at work. Maybe it's talking with a friend or a neighbor about how some book you just read helped you imagine a better world. Maybe you'll encourage your students to use texts as tactics as a class project. Or you could apply for grants, team up with community organizations, create a website, or set up a reading series to draw attention to the issues that matter most to you.

On the first page I called this book a set of blueprints. Do what you will with them. Imitate, remix, or—inspired by the tactical readers whose stories I've shared—invent wholly new strategies. Whoever you are, I think there are ideas here for you. And whatever you do with them—whatever you've already done—I'd love to hear about it.[1]

Of course this book isn't *just* blueprints. Throughout I have been making an argument against a particular common sense understanding of literature. In the United States in the early twenty-first century, literature is imagined to be increasingly marginal: "dead" is the common metaphor. Sometimes, for emphasis, this tragic death is juxtaposed with a (mythical) past when literature was at the vital center of public life. To this, our current common sense adds one more paradoxical element. Literature's vitality, on the rare occasion it's noted, is visible only in private ways; it's deeply personal and, as in Timothy Aubry's compelling cultural diagnosis, therapeutic.[2] Thus, literature is really great, but it's dead or dying, except (maybe) when it's read for emotional sustenance.

I'm skeptical. At least in part because this common sense is hardly new: much of it dates at least to Victorian platitudes about how culture (mostly the culture of rich white people) might "improve" everyone (but especially those people who aren't rich or white). It's hardly the only common sense based on racist, classist assumptions we've inherited from the Victorians. And even if that genealogy doesn't bother you, I hope I've shown how this common sense is, if nothing else, limiting. It creates a set of conditions under which we—often without realizing it—approach the books we read. If it's common sense to assume that literature is dead for most everyone except a chosen few who pursue it for their own private (or professional) reasons, it's easy to privilege esoteric reading strategies (no one else is reading anyway!) or to read in solitary ways (no one else is reading anyway!). These ways of reading have benefits, but they also serve to deepen a reader's isolation. That's disempowering in itself, and it also reinforces that isolating common sense and leads us to overlook precisely the kind of collaborative political work literature is capable of facilitating.

The stories I've been sharing here run counter to that common sense in most every way. I've been showing how literature is not dead but vital. Literature is not elitist; it belongs to many different types of people. Literature is not just a therapeutic elixir, but a tool for our collective remaking of our world. When you use texts as tactics, literature doesn't change just *your* life, it can change *our* lives. And these tactical readers—my students Addison, Lindsay, Sheree, Tarale, and Eleshia; Jon Hart, Cynthia Landrum, Judy Szink, and Kate Lambert Lee in Jackson; Mayor Ragsdale, Sara Baker, Angela Cash, Loida Velazquez in Knoxville; the many anonymous readers and republishers after September 11—really are working to change *our* lives. I hope my retelling has done justice to their ambitions and has given due credit to their successes. They show us literature's power in a new light.

But to change a common sense, especially when it has deep historical roots, takes lots of work. The more people use texts as tactics—not just read (or write) scholarly books about it—the more common the practices become and the more literature's potential to change the world becomes something more than potential. None of that happens without more readers like us using texts as tactics.

And that's my real hope. I want to end on lines borrowed from the final page of Russell Banks's fascinating and messy early novel *Continental Drift* (1985). Banks's admonition holds significance both for the readers I've written about here and for the readers I hope they inspire: "Sabotage and subversion, then, are this book's objectives. Go, my book, and help destroy the world as it is."[3]

Reading as Collective Action, I'm afraid, is no destroyer of worlds. But attending to how readers use texts as tactics does offer a key to understanding and unlocking the powerful, and all too often hidden, political alchemy brought into play in the interaction between texts, readers, publics, institutions, and laws. That potential is, I believe, the basis for the political work all readers are capable of. But it's only with our help that books can destroy the world—and rebuild a better one in its place.

Notes

PROLOGUE

1. Boyte, *Everyday Politics*, 4, xvii. Another of Boyte's definitions for everyday politics: "people of different views, interests, and backgrounds interacting in order to accomplish some task" (xi–xii).

2. Fraser, "Reframing Justice," 73. My emphases. In other recent work, particularly "Abnormal Justice," Fraser explains in great detail why traditional models of justice—nation states, courts, and laws—are inadequate today and why, in a world of highly mobile populations and disagreements about what constitutes justice at all, this multidimensional framework for justice is necessary. For some people, recognition *is* justice; for others, nothing short of redistribution will serve as redress. I'll work through these terms with Fraser throughout, giving examples and drawing out her definitions.

3. You'll see that definition again. I think Sun Tzu's *Art of War* may be the ur-definition of tactics. There he notes tactics are best not repeated but "regulated by the infinite variety of circumstances" (252). In English departments, though, Certeau's complementary definition is certainly better known: a means of resistance in a highly stratified power structure, a "use" that runs contrary to presumptive—or programmatic—uses (30). I detail these ideas more completely in the final chapter.

4. Margaret Post et al., "Introducing Next-Generation Engagement," 2.

CHAPTER 1

1. Carter and Barringer, "In Patriotic Time, Dissent Is Muted."

2. See, for instance, Nguyen, *We Are All Suspects Now* (2005); Welch, *Scapegoats of September 11* (2006); and the Leadership Conference on Civil Rights' exhaustive

report: "Wrong Then, Wrong Now: Racial Profiling before & after September 11, 2001." For more stories, look at Verhovek, "Americans Give In to Race Profiling"; Toner, "Civil Liberty vs. Security."

3. Bush, "Freedom at War with Fear."

4. Dinitia Smith, "In Shelley or Auden, in the Sonnet or Free Verse, the Eerily Intimate Power of Poetry to Console"; Schmich, "Poetry Soothes the Soul in These Painful Days."

5. Johnson and Merians, *Poetry after 9/11: An Anthology of New York Poets*, ix.

6. "Open Letter from the Metropolitan Museum of Art"; D. Smith, "In Shelley or Auden"; Trebay, "At a Loss and Craving Order"; Johnson and Merians, *Poetry after 9/11*, ix.

7. Mary Schmich, "Poetry Soothes the Soul."

8. Trebay: "Poetry suddenly appeared all over." Dinitia Smith: "Improvised memorials often conceived around poems sprang up all over the city, in store windows, at bus stops, in Washington Square Park, Brooklyn Heights and elsewhere"; and Billy Collins said he was "inundated with poems from friends." Eric McHenry notes, "Tragedy sends people to poetry." Sven Bikerts puts it more poetically: "A poem that's been everywhere in the air these last days." S. Smith: "Auden, Blake, Dickinson[,] the musty musings of the great ones glow bright from poetry Web sites and list serves trafficked the past month by users clicking for comfort."

9. I use "anthology" most explicitly in its root sense, "a collection of flowers" (Ramazani, "Writing Life"), though it is also appropriate, as I'll discuss below, in its more contemporary, Norton-anthology sense.

10. A good overview of these questions comes in Amy Gutmann's introduction to *Multiculturalism: Examining the Politics of Recognition.*

11. Even Charles Taylor's famous—and hardly literary—essay, "The Politics of Recognition," uses the canon as a metaphor for inclusion in the polity.

12. See Fraser, "Abnormal Justice."

13. Burt, "'September 1, 1939' Revisited," 534.

14. The poem was falsely identified as "an American-Indian poem" (D. Smith).

15. "Open Letter"; Milton Esterow, "From the Editor and Publisher," *ARTnews*, November 2001, accessed 5 March 2009; "Artpourri," *ARTtalk*, accessed 5 March 2009.

16. D. Smith, "In Shelley or Auden"; Oliveri, "Emotions Are Shared in Library Gatherings."

17. See Gwiazda, "The Aesthetics of Politics / The Politics of Aesthetics," 446–448.

18. See Hengen Fox, "Poetry, Recognition, and Redistribution: The September 11 Chronocanon," *American Literature* (2015).

19. Fowler, *Kinds of Literature*, 214.

20. Bourdieu, *Distinction*, 44.

21. Guillory, *Cultural Capital*, 30–32. My emphasis.

22. In another context, one might argue that particularly well-respected anthologies materialize the canon. Anthologizing is, as Jahan Ramazani (himself an anthologist) argues, "one of the more effective processes we have for shaping and recognizing literary worth."

23. Bernstein, "Poetry's Insights on Pain and Joy," E1.

24. Robert Herrick, "To the Virgins, to Make Much of Time," *Poetryfoundation .org*, accessed 10 September 2015. https://www.poetryfoundation.org/poems-and -poets/poems/detail/46546.

25. Zagajewski, "Try to Praise."

26. Auden, "September 1, 1939," 801–803.

27. Auden, before repudiating the entire poem later in life, would change that final line to "We must love one another *and* die"—a slightly less comforting thought (my emphasis). While the poem has a fascinating textual history, I want to note that this extra-textual history is inscribed in few of the poem's post–September 11 republications. For more, see Mendelson, *Later Auden*, 74–79.

28. Shakespeare, *The Sonnets*, 58.

29. Shelley, *Shelley's Poetry and Prose*, 14.

30. Auden, 802–803.

31. Shakespeare, *The Sonnets*, 58.

32. Moore, *The Complete Poems*, 95.

33. Amichai, *Selected Poetry*, 1. The website, *Moby Lives*, is still there, if you're curious: http://www.mobylives.com/Ostriker_anthology.html.

34. "Poems after the Attack"; Rich, *Dark Fields of the Republic*, 4.

35. Oliveri, "Emotions Are Shared in Library Gatherings," A4.

36. S. Smith, "Seeking Solace in the Words," F1.

37. Price, "The New American War: True Patriotism or Blind Loyalty?"

38. Rukeyser, *The Collected Poems*, 430.

39. My emphases. These poems—particularly in their use of the first-person plural—map closely onto the type of poem Robert von Hallberg has recently named "civic": poems that aspire to speak to or for a certain class of people, particularly, in von Hallberg's argument, the upper-middle-class intelligentsia. See von Hallberg, *Lyric Powers*, 72ff.

40. Bush, "Freedom at War with Fear." http://usatoday30.usatoday.com/news/nation/2001/09/21/bush-text.htm.

41. Consider, for instance, the contrast between Auden, who like many other Western intellectuals, had been drawn to Communism in the mid-1930s, and Moore. The latter was "strongly conservative," at one point writing an ode in praise of Herbert Hoover. See Molesworth, *Marianne Moore*, 259.

42. Hamod, "After the Funeral of Assam Hamady," 288.

43. Ibid., 289, 290.

44. Ibid., 289.

45. Ibid., 291.

46. The Perishable Press, based in Mt. Horeb, Wisconsin, published twenty copies of Hamod's poem on September 26, 1971, "the date that day equals night" (*After the Funeral of Assam Hamady*, Mt. Horeb, WI: Perishable Press, 1971).

47. Hamod, 291.

48. Ibid., 289.

49. Ibid., 290.

50. Hamod, Letter to the Editor, *Los Angeles Times*, December 1, 2001.

51. Matt Welch, "The Lie of 'Dissent,' and the Curious Case of Palestinian-Enthusiast Sam Hamod," Mattwelch.com, accessed 2 October 2010; for Hamod on TV, see BET Tonight, "America on Alert."

52. "Poet Sam Hamod Reads One of His Poems."

53. Lorna Dee Cervantes, "Palestine," *About.com: Poems after the Attack*, accessed 2 October 2010, http://poetry.about.com/library/weekly/aa091201c.htm. As "Palestine" is a single-page poem, further textual references will not be cited with individual notes.

54. A similar question ends Darwish's "Psalm 2" (1980). The earlier poem sets up a split between death by physical violence and death by, in essence, ideology. Darwish would seem to make us choose—bulldozers and bullets or the Zionist ideology that underpins their onslaught? This, of course, is an extratextual

foray, not at all obvious to the casual reader of the poem. And for this analysis, I'm limiting myself to what a casual reader might encounter in this anthology.

55. In this, Hamod and Cervantes are hardly alone in the anthology. Ginsberg's "Kaddish," in the lines quoted on About.com, draws on diverse religious traditions ("the Hebrew Anthem, or the Buddhist Book of Answers") as well as global political solidarities ("the great dream of Me or China, or you and a phantom Russia"). See Ginsberg, *Collected Poems*, 217.

56. See, for examples, Mearsheimer and Walt, *The Israel Lobby*, especially 111–150.

57. With cover art, not incidentally, by Emory Douglas—the former minister of culture for the Black Panther Party—whose visual style is closely aligned with the Black Power movement.

58. Baraka, *Somebody Blew Up America*, 52.

59. Ibid., 49. Not a first for Baraka. The Anti-Defamation League has attacked Baraka's anti-Semitism before. While many of the charges there fall into the trap of equating anti-Zionist rhetoric with anti-Semitism, they also nail down ugly quotes from early in Baraka's career, calling for "dagger poems in the slimy bellies / of the owner-jews" and "Another bad poem cracking / steel knuckles in a jewlady's mouth" (*Black Magic* 116, 117). These most damning quotes come from Baraka's 1960s, black nationalist awakening and predate his *Village Voice* piece, "Confessions of a Former Anti-Semite," where he repudiates anti-Semitism.

60. Ibid., 49. As the controversy escalated, a budget shortfall was discovered, and New Jersey thought it wise to terminate Baraka's $10,000-a-year position to save money (*Somebody Blew Up America*, 52–54).

61. Ibid., 41–43.

62. Ibid., 50. My emphasis.

63. Fraser and Honneth, *Redistribution or Recognition*, 36. My emphasis.

64. Young, *Inclusion and Democracy*, 56. Young's "communicative democracy" cites features of language—emotion, figures of speech, symbolism, rhetorical attention to audience—often explicitly associated with literary works. I'll harken back to her work throughout this book.

65. Billeaudeaux, et al. in *Media in an American Crisis: Studies of September 11, 2001*, 61. See also Chang, *Silencing Political Dissent*, 93.

66. Felski, *Uses of Literature*, 18. I say more about this tendency in chapter 4.

67. Fraser, "Abnormal Justice," 402.

68. Fraser, "Reframing Justice," 75.

69. And it took a few hundred years to get even this close. I'm using such cautious language here because of—to take one example—the millions of undocumented residents of the United States who are part of our polity in the loose sense but are guaranteed few legal protections.

70. For instance, the admittedly literary/academic confines of the Buffalo Poetics listserv, whose post–September 11 verse commentaries are chronicled by Susan M. Schultz in *A Poetics of Impasse*, 209–216.

71. Eric McHenry, "Auden on Bin Laden"; Ramos-Mrosovsky, "Exposing the Hate Speech of the Radical Fringe," *Daily Princetonian*, November 15, 2001.

72. Such evidence is, perhaps necessarily, partial. This is not a well-maintained archive, but a mess of circulatory practices by a range of people. Given their marginality, even such fragments indicate a wide circulation. If I were really discussing only a few e-mails and conversations, I never would have found such documents. I'm echoing Robert Darnton. His objects of study, too, are fragmentary. But they would never be found at all if they were not "a small part of a huge literature of protest" (*Poetry and the Police*, 120–121).

73. Trebay, "At a Loss and Craving Order."

74. "More Grim Milestones for the *New York Times*," SeekingAlpha.com, last modified 9 March 2010. Accessed 10 September 2015.

75. Such assertions about the way words transform public space, particularly in New York City, echo David Henkin's *City Reading: Written Words and Public Spaces in Antebellum New York* (1998).

76. Ruhe, "A Dose of Painting, Poetry, and Music."

77. Massing, "Press Watch," 197–201; Butler, Precarious Life, 36–37. In light of continued instances of media malfeasance greasing the wheels of war (e.g., Judith Miller's reporting on weapons of mass destruction for the *New York Times* in 2003), it is difficult *not* to imagine something of a direct line between the Bush administration's policy decisions and the output of editors and publishers at various strata of mass media.

78. D. Smith, "In Shelley or Auden."

79. "Arguments through the Ages."

80. Sarah, "Poetry Has Words for Times like These."

81. Trebay, "At a Loss and Craving Order."

82. "To Our Readers."

83. See, for instance, Poncavage, "When People Turn to Poetry"; Kakutani, "Rituals for Grieving Extend Past Tradition into Public Displays."

84. Poncavage, "When People Turn to Poetry."

85. Circulating in these ways, poems reclaim a bit of what Habermas so admired—at least in his early work—in the long-gone public sphere of the eighteenth-century European bourgeoisie: a type of critical publicity. Individually, the poems speak back to racist, nationalist narratives; taken together as an anthology, the voice is even more emphatic.

86. I'm rehashing Nancy Fraser's critique of Habermas's earliest formulation of the "public sphere" (from his dissertation): in short, that the public sphere is always exclusive, often oppressive. The space we often declare "public" isn't available to everyone. I can't help but note, though, that this anthology does speak to Fraser's concerns quite well. Not only is the anthology inclusive of diverse voices—including poets of different races, genders, classes—but because of contemporary mass media's capacity, these poems reach far more people across far greater distances and differences. These poems were "everywhere" and were representing diverse realities, to huge swaths of the population, both those who recognized these experiences as familiar and could feel solidarity and those for whom such experiences were neither experientially familiar nor (in other parts of the media) visible.

87. Fraser, "Rethinking the Public Sphere," 62. Fraser's use of "hegemonic" here seems to draw on a limited reading of the word's Gramscian sense—a limitation not uncommon in contemporary critical writing. See, for instance, Brennan, *Wars of Position*, 233–235.

88. There are few instances of poetry being called marginal or ineffectual (which contrasts with most contemporary mass media representations of poetry). It's true that poetry's power, in this context, is often attributed to Arnoldian notions of art as improving or to a more generalized sense of poetry and art as affectively comforting. One republication of Auden's poem (in the *Baltimore Sun*) is headlined: "A Poem from September 1939 Reaches Out to September 2001." The poem is figured as the affective compatriot, reaching out from the past to offer comfort and understanding to the present. Yet the article's author, Michael Collier, immediately points out the poem's "power . . . does not lie in pieties of patriotism or revolution, but rather in its affirming skepticism."

89. Fraser, "Reframing Justice," 75.

90. "Bridging" is one of the powers of communicative action Habermas discusses in detail in *Between Facts and Norms*. It's how language (especially liter-

ary language, I'd argue) connects people across difference (374). More on this in chapter 4.

91. Baraka, *Somebody Blew Up America*; Auden, "September 1, 1939"; Shakespeare, Sonnet 64; Rukeyser, *Collected Poems*; Cervantes, "Palestine."

92. W. B. Yeats, "Meditations in the Time of Civil War," *About.com: Poems after the Attack*, accessed 2 October 2010; Heaney, "The Cure at Troy" in D. Smith, "In Shelley or Auden"; Moore, *The Complete Poems*, 95.

93. As Fraser notes in "Rethinking the Public Sphere": "Subordinate groups sometimes cannot find the right voice or words to express their thoughts, and when they do, they discover they are not heard" (64).

94. Marx, "The Eighteenth Brumaire of Louis Bonaparte" in *Later Political Writings*, 117.

95. Ibid., 32.

96. Fraser, "Reframing Justice," 73.

97. Ellison, "The Humanities and the Public Soul," 118.

CHAPTER 2

1. Dry, "John Steinbeck Would Love This Recession."

2. To both, I also provided more open-ended opportunities to draw connections between the Depression-era text and the "Great Recession" of 2009. To the facilitators, I asked specific questions about how they became involved in the Big Read, how facilitating events such as these differed from other book clubs.

3. "History," *Community Action Agency*, accessed 14 September 2009. http://www.caajlh.org/about/overview.

4. Lee, *Faces of Poverty*, 6.

5. This blending of rational social service and aesthetic purpose again evokes Iris Marion Young's calls for a politics that integrates more diverse publics by using more diverse modes of communication. I discuss Young's work in more detail in chapter 1.

6. "National Endowment for the Arts Announces the Big Read." By 2008, the NEA was spending over $1.5 million yearly on The Big Read.

7. "About the Big Read," *National Endowment for the Arts*, accessed 23 July 2009. Wording on the site has been revised since then. http://www.neabigread.org/about.php.

8. Ibid. Wording has been revised.

9. Hart, interview.

10. Cummings, "Big Read Book Strikes a Chord."

11. Steinbeck, *Grapes of Wrath,* 285.

12. Ibid., 288.

13. Benson, "'To Tom, Who Lived It': John Steinbeck and the Man from Weedpatch," 160.

14. Ibid., 160–163.

15. Ibid., 163–164.

16. Steinbeck, "The Harvest Gypsies," 1006.

17. Benson, "To Tom," 164–165.

18. Ibid., 176.

19. Steinbeck, *Grapes*, 288.

20. Sayles, interview.

21. Claibourne, interview.

22. Volk, interview.

23. Hart, interview.

24. It seems fair to note, though, that the poetry reading, held at the high school, was mandatory for a good number of the attendees.

25. Cummings, "Big Read Book Strikes a Chord." Under-attendance at the Services Fair may have had other causes as well, according to Jessie Murray: its location was accidentally not noted on some promotional material and, worse, that Saturday was one of the first warm days after a Michigan winter.

26. *Grapes,* 316. This refusal was real in the 1930s, as well. FSA campers "would refuse to avail themselves of food or even medicine offered to them free by the government if they had any choice in the matter" (Benson 176).

27. Famously, at the 1934 Soviet Writer's Congress, where the party forcefully advocated for "socialist realism," the writer was defined as the "engineer of human souls." For more, see Kemp-Welch, *Stalin and the Literary Intelligentsia, 1928–39*.

28. "About the NEA Big Read," my emphasis. Wording on the site has been revised since then.

29. "City of Bridgeport," my emphasis.

30. Oxford English Dictionary, 3rd ed., s.v. "community."

31. Ibid.

32. "About the NEA Big Read."

33. *Reading at Risk*. After this survey, the NEA was well aware of differences, particularly based on race, class, and gender. *Reading at Risk* notes the gaps between whites (about half of whom were readers) and African Americans or Hispanics were large and growing. Literary reading was reported by 51.4 percent of whites, 37.1 percent of African Americans, and 26.5 percent of Hispanic Americans (x). Though education is not a perfect cipher for class, it's noteworthy that 66.7 percent of people with college degrees reported reading, contrasted with 37.7 percent of those with high school degrees (xi).

It's worth noting that the above quote emphasizes "citizens," which ties inclusion explicitly to national status. The Big Read is about the United States in some ineffable way—particularly ineffable given that the Big Read's list has recently expanded to include three non-US authors: Tolstoy (*The Death of Ivan Ilyich* [1886]), Naguib Mahfouz (*The Thief and the Dogs* [1961]), and a collection of Mexican short fiction.

34. Gioia, "Prepared Statement of Dana Gioia."

35. Long, *Book Clubs: Women and the Uses of Reading in Everyday Life*, xvi.

36. Linsey Howie argues that such reading practices allow readers to "play with, or assert different ideas, or adopt different subject positions in the presence of others," which helps them throw off "confining self-representations" and offers "novel ways of perceiving [themselves] as . . . subject[s]-in-process."

37. Velasquez, interview.

38. Sayles, interview.

39. Carler, interview.

40. Baker, interview. This story was reported by Sara Baker, a Big Read co-chair.

41. Habermas, *Reason and the Rationalization of Society*, 285–286.

42. Habermas calls this the "grammar of forms of life": a clunky phrase, but one that helps illustrate how such practices can structure our life the way grammar structures our language (*Lifeworld and System*, 392).

43. Szink, interview.

44. Interestingly, Harvey Teres, who also studied a Big Read group reading *Grapes*, reports very different conclusions. His study "revealed a troubling absence of concern for the pleasures of the text or, indeed, for any of the key issues that have engaged discerning readers of Steinbeck's novel since its publication in 1939" (6). Teres provides an example of a particularly scholarly mode of

reading for politics: Teres wants to find the book in public—a good baseline for politics—but he wants it to be read in "discerning" (code, I think, for academic) terms, a way of reading that is inherently less public.

45. I feel this particularly as someone who makes a living trying to create spaces for such insight in my classroom. How remarkable for those participants whose lives seldom allow them access to such interactions—those, for instance, who never had a chance to attend (or finish) college, those who just miss taking courses—to find them. More than one of my interviewees fondly recalled participating in the Big Read as like going back to college again. "It was really fun to be with a college professor who can deconstruct a book again. . . . I was just overwhelmed by the discussion . . . just getting in to a literary conversation," said Mary Pom Claiborne—whose *Grapes* reading group was led by University of Tennessee English professor Mary Papke. And she was not the only participant in such a group. Indeed, Cynthia Landrum, whom I'll discuss below, is also an adjunct professor in Jackson.

46. Long, *Book Clubs*, xiv, 88.

47. Of my twenty conversations, three quarters were with women. Perhaps more strikingly, not one was under the age of thirty. These proportions are evident in Long's work as well: mostly women, whose average age is fifty-one (89).

48. The book club, then, presents a similar situation to Stanley Fish's "reading community." Fish, in a move similar to that of the Big Read, conveniently elides "community" with "college classroom," so as to avoid discussing all the attendant exclusions built into the college classroom. And, while the book clubs sponsored by the Big Read do not have applications or give grades, many are—culturally, racially, economically, educationally—not unlike colleges.

49. Szink, interview.

50. A notion that—as the failure of the FSA camps indicates—is not wholly accurate. Making transformative change has never been easy.

51. Jane Volk, the retired teacher who reminded me that many "things that are right—they don't happen until the government gets in there," is one of the few people whose book group includes people with different opinions: "My book club is conservative. There's only two or three of us who are not." In discussing *Grapes*, they, as they have in the past, "drop [contentious issues] rather than have conflict. Actually, I probably could argue most of 'em. I'm not gonna change their minds. Why confuse 'em with facts?" Amusing, but disconcerting in that rather than engage in conversation aimed at changing minds, Volk simply keeps the peace at the cost of deeper discussion about the causes of the Joads' suffer-

ing. Not only does this curtail discussion, but it also potentially limits the development of empathy and (obviously) action.

52. Steinbeck, *The Grapes of Wrath*. Notably, this fictional reimagining of community produced its own, rather remarkable, community shortly after its publication in March 1939. The book sold over 430,000 copies that year alone and became the talk of the nation, discussed at town hall meetings throughout California, in newspapers in many states, and in letters—including famous missives from Eleanor Roosevelt and others (Parini 276; Wartzman 7).

53. Putnam, *Bowling Alone: The Collapse and Revival of American Community*.

54. Ragsdale, interview.

55. Crandall, interview.

56. Claiborne, interview.

57. I'm describing here what Habermas calls a "lifeworld," the "background convictions" that enable conversation and collaboration. This lifeworld is constructed by everything from language and communicative norms to ontological orientation (*The Theory of Communicative Action, Volume 1*, 70).

58. Landrum, "Grapes of Wrath," sermon, 6, 9.

59. Landrum, interview.

60. "CommUnity ForUm," promotional poster by the Universalist Unitarian Church of East Liberty, Jackson, Michigan, 2009.

61. Of course, these public spaces are not all the same. The authority of the pulpit, for instance, is very different from the librarian's desk; the "public" nature of a book club watched on TV is quite different from a public forum. And I want to be clear: publicity does not make anything inherently political. But publicity allows these ideas to reach more (and more diverse) readers than are included in the typical book club (or, to name an even more exclusive space, the classroom).

62. Hart, interview.

63. Cash, interview.

64. While the texts themselves are not, I would say, redistributive on the same scale as, say, welfare or a food pantry, they were passed out for free. And it's certainly noteworthy that both *depict* redistribution: food giveaways, community agencies.

65. Or, to put it in a more Habermasian register, a "network of communicative actions that branch out through social space and historical time" (*Between Facts and Norms*, 80).

66. For example, many of my interviewees reported discussing the novel with their spouses or children who did not actively participate.

67. Baker, interview.

68. Lambert Lee, interview.

69. Volk, interview.

70. Millard, interview.

71. Landrum, interview.

72. While *The Grapes of Wrath*, particularly during the "Great Recession," offers obvious grounding for such work, many books offer a similar platform. Of those deemed appropriate by the Big Read, the text of *To Kill a Mockingbird* is thematically rich enough to provide launching points for such tactical intervention anywhere in the United States today, with its charged questions about racism and the judicial system. To take another example, perhaps *Fahrenheit 451* (1953) could launch a town into discussions about responses to NSA eavesdropping or into plans to develop sustainable practices in promoting reading among low-literacy groups.

73. Sun Tzu, *Art of War*, 152.

74. Ellison: "Public scholarship in the arts and humanities most differs from standard academic practice through its explicit hopefulness" ("The Humanities and the Public Soul," 115).

CHAPTER 3

1. Fitzgerald et al. in "The Centrality of Engagement" find these as key terms among varied practitioners of public engagement: "cut across the missions of teaching, research, and service," "reciprocal and mutually beneficial," and "embrace the processes and values of a civil democracy" (23).

2. For an overview, see Rhoads, *Freedom's Web: Student Activism in the Age of Cultural Diversity*, especially the first chapter.

3. I made this argument in an essay called "Teaching (Is Not) Activism." There, I described the sometimes self-congratulatory ways in which teachers (including myself!) see their work as political, without ever seeing any political results. I described an American literature class where I taught students about how others had used texts as tactics, but ultimately felt I hadn't done much political work. For more, including lots of specific examples, see that essay.

4. Thanks, Rachel Stevens!

5. Others teach courses like this as "The Literature of Everyday Life" or "Class Fictions." See a thorough list of syllabi at the Center for Working-Class Studies: http://cwcs.ysu.edu/teaching/syllabus-library.

6. It's worth noting that this is a doubly complex question at an institution designed by its very nature to enroll more nontraditional (i.e., not privileged, often working-class) students. I'll deal with this dynamic a bit more in talking about the assignment's structure.

7. All quotations from the assignment sheet and from student work in this chapter are in my possession. For more details, please contact me: nicholashengen@gmail.com.

8. See Thaler and Sunstein, *Nudge: Improving Decisions about Health, Wealth, and Happiness* (2008).

9. See Miles, "Get Up, Stand Up: Teaching Civil Disobedience in the Literature Classroom," and Mollis, "Servicing Reading: Community Work and the Revaluation of Literary Study."

10. As always, some students push beyond these structural limits. One day when Eleshia and Tarale were doing interviews, Eleshia's childcare fell through—so she took her toddler along. That kind of dedication is a familiar story to most community college faculty. Still, it seems to me to be more than an instructor can ethically demand of students with so many other demands on their time.

11. Marx, "The Eighteenth Brumaire of Louis Bonaparte" in *Later Political Writings*, 32.

12. Steve's band can (and should) be heard here: https://www.youtube.com/watch?v=15h_GVsftOw.

13. In three years of teaching the course, I've had only one student—an exceptionally talented one—really fight the assignment (and its tensions with traditional academic expectations) to a draw. In the end, she wrote a paper that focused on materialist questions about the writing and production of literature, but at our final meeting when other students were singing songs or playing videos or projecting images, she couldn't really participate.

14. They also posted their survey on their Facebook pages, but they got only six responses there.

15. It would certainly be interesting to do a follow up with those interviewees—or to meditate on what made another respondent name Marilyn Manson as her example of working-class literature.

16. Even if, in class, we didn't all have the same definition—we had two long and (alas) inconclusive conversations about whether or not donuts are working-class, for instance—we all were willing to discuss the term without casting aspersions or shutting down.

17. Such critiques range from the early Frankfurt School to the Situationists to David Graeber's *Debt: The First 5,000 Years* (2011).

18. They also recognized that the role of "expert" is hardly as infallible as it might seem from the outside. Their interviews showed them that many people off campus knew things—about class and literature, for instance—they hadn't learned in their reading or in our class. As an example, Tarale and Eleshia acknowledge unfamiliarity with Ayn Rand or George Orwell, who were both named by survey respondents.

19. Freire, *Pedagogy of the Oppressed*, 61.

20. This point ties into the well-established line of critiques of Habermas's Theory of Communicative Action—in short, that Habermas idealizes speech, that situations of equitable exchange are impossible. See, for instance, Jean-Jacques Lecercle mocking Habermas's "irenic philosophy of language based on the co-operation implicit in interlocution" (917).

21. *Rough Crossing* can be found at: http://rough-crossing.tumblr.com/. I won't note the link in subsequent references.

22. This is true, of course, of all Tumblr pages. Initially, Lindsay had attempted to craft the group's own theme, though they ultimately purchased the one they used from Tumblr. They made a good choice in that the simple background draws the eye to their content.

23. The theme of gender in the Tumblr—while not explicitly announced—is unmistakable, not only in the Lange/Trent page, but in its stark contrast with the masculinity (both visible and imagined) of the lumberjacks that dominate the site's pages. Sheree and Lindsay (who is now minoring in gender/women's studies at a nearby university) were certainly aware of this.

24. And while it's not particularly important for the assignment, I want to emphasize they also suggest an awareness of (if not a fluency in) the conventions of academic research. Despite the project being totally nontraditional by academic standards, the students still recognized the need for documentation—maybe even (is it too much to suggest?) the value of such practices.

25. See, for instance, the massive compilation of images depicting "lumberjack style" on Pinterest.com.

26. In fact, because this is not a face-to-face discussion, *Rough Crossing* is able to provide more information—and allow more contemplative reception.

27. Economic redistribution—the "distribution of resources and wealth"—has "supplied the paradigm case for most theorizing about social justice for the past 150 years" (Fraser and Honneth, 7). And I've mostly used "redistribution" in this sense. Yet part of these paradigmatic movements for social justice (the 150-year arc Fraser and Honneth allude to in that quote aligns well with movements for both workers' rights and women's rights) was more than just higher wages or calls for women's control of their own property and money. Both movements called for the redistribution of knowledge: literacy via free, public education, for instance. Redistribution—a topic for a longer project—is complex (Fraser and Honneth, 36).

28. Campus Compact, *Creating a Culture of Assessment*, 2, 6.

29. I want to emphasize that I did consider constructing the course as a service learning opportunity and began to work through all the difficult problems so familiar to service-learning instructors: how to find the right community partners; how to match the coursework with the service component; how to encourage students to develop their own thoughts and practices.

30. Quoted in Mitchell, "Traditional vs. Critical Service-Learning," 51.

31. Colby et al., *Educating for Democracy*, 5. "A review of college-level service learning programs—one of the fastest growing forms of civic education on American campuses—found that among six hundred programs, more than half involved" those activities just listed.

32. On charity, see Morton, "The Irony of Service"; on class as an "us/them" scenario, see Henry, "I Can Never Turn My Back on That." More generally my concerns here echo many of Henry Giroux's critiques of higher education and its preference for "pedagogies that confirm the autonomous individual" rather than teach common goods (*Impure Acts*, 12).

33. As David D. Blouin and Evelyn M. Perry have pointed out, the volume of research on how service learning benefits students far outweighs studies of how students' service benefits partner organizations. While Blouin and Perry see some benefits, their article also cites some hazards that I worried about.

34. Boyte, "The Necessity of Politics," 82. I'm echoing Morton's well-known critique of the "continuum" of service here, as well; as he rightly points out, there's scant evidence that, on its own, service learning moves students any closer to political activism.

35. Mitchell, "Traditional vs. Critical," 50, 62.

36. Mitchell, 58. Awfully Habermasian-sounding terms, I have to note.

37. And, incidentally, this is one of Habermas's concerns about literature's role in communicative action. This is why my use of him as a core thinker in this project is complicated, though, as I've argued elsewhere, important. See more of this argument in the second section of chapter 4 and in my "A Habermasian Literary Criticism."

38. I would seem to be evidencing concerns voiced by Laurie Grobman and others that community engagement "can too easily encourage narrow interpretations of literature to fit or explain real-world situations, . . . thereby erasing the complexities of literary interpretation" (2). Yet as I've articulated here, so much of our "sociological" discussion is also grounded in analysis of literary texts; and my students' projects also incorporate literary thinking and practice. In short, you can do both—in the classroom and in the world. That is one of this book's central contentions.

39. Mitchell, "Traditional vs. Critical," 55.

40. I have to admit, for instance, that their work does stay, at least partly, on campus. While outward facing—aiming at and available to off-campus audiences—I was the students' main interlocutor in developing their projects; their main collaborators were other students, faculty, and administrators; the institutional skills they learned were mostly learned in campus networks. Service learning placements do solve this problem, though at (as I've been discussing) other costs.

41. Mitchell, "Traditional vs. Critical," 60.

42. As college teaching becomes increasingly casualized and, thus, increasingly transient—whether we're talking about "freeway fliers" who teach at three schools on any given day or faculty with more stable placements who jump around the country (or globe) pursuing better jobs for much of their professional lives—the disconnection of the professoriate from the communities their institutions serve is an important consideration. Faculty-community partner collaboration is hard and getting harder.

43. Just under 75 percent of the community partners studied by Brenda Bushouse in 2005 indicated that they preferred "transactional" rather than "transformative" service-learning relationships. And that study examined placement of graduate students, who have more skills in the areas of their placement than undergrads! Bushouse cites a handful of other studies with similar conclusions. The alternative, in which students would do more analysis and, for instance, shape programming, is too much work for the community organization.

44. Colby et al., *Educating for Democracy*, 8.

45. Ibid., 13.

46. Ibid., 18.

47. Ibid.

48. I'm quoting the title of Longo, Kiesa, and Battistoni's essay "The Future of the Academy with Students as Colleagues," which is part of the manifesto-collection *Publicly Engaged Scholars: Next-Generation Engagement* (2016). I'll have more to say about their work in chapter 4.

49. Sheffield, "Service Learning," 11.

50. Certeau, *The Practice of Everyday Life*, 37.

51. For more on Young, see the slightly longer discussion of her in chapter 1; or see my more detailed discussion of Young and Habermas in Hengen Fox, "A Habermasian Literary Criticism," 248–249.

52. As Ed Zlotkowski (himself a literature professor) has pointed out, the American Association of Higher Education and Accreditation's twenty-two-volume series on service learning in the disciplines doesn't include a single volume on literature.

53. Kara Mollis's assignment—where students "perform[ed] a community service that related to their particular interpretations of the novels' representations of their selected issues or related problems"—offers some hope on this count (54). One of her students mentored a Girl Scout troop, reading literature with them. However, most of Mollis's other examples of student work are less directly literary.

54. A good example of this major challenge shows up in Kevin Guerrieri's "*Leer y escribir la frontera.*" Guierrieri describes a course that involves reading border narratives in Spanish: the service component is one day at a shelter for migrants. No doubt students make connections and gain insights, but how authentic? How literary?

55. If you've ever been on the wrong side of a fight with a librarian about an ILL request, you know why I use an exclamation point.

56. One more example: a different student of mine, while filming interviews in public, was stopped by the police for not having a permit. She not only learned about a (fairly silly) law, but also developed her critique of it as she devised ways to continue her interviews without police interference.

57. And while in-class groups can often be a product of pairing with old friends from high school, both of these groups are marked by their diversity: Sheree

was older than Addison and Lindsay combined; Tarale scored As in most of her classes, while Eleshia had barely passed my introductory writing course the previous term. These groups, then, despite being (at one level) homogeneously "college students," were also collaborations among diverse humans.

58. And, again, this serves to emphasize the value of Habermas's theory of communicative action: these examples of communicative action aren't yet impacting laws or even civil society. Yet, without them, no one (except millionaires) could ever hope to intervene at those levels.

59. Admittedly, not a lot of research covers this topic, though as Lucia d'Arlach, Bernadette Sánchez, and Rachel Feuer note in a recent issue of the *Michigan Journal of Community Service Learning,* there's a reasonable explanation for that: "Administrators of community-based (generally nonprofit and small) organizations are unlikely to repudiate or jeopardize a partnership with a well-funded university by making negative comments in a university-sponsored survey" (5). In off-the-record conversations with friends who work at community organizations that use service learners, I've heard many frustrated mumbles about students who show up late (or not at all) or who lack the skills (practical, intellectual, emotional) to do the work.

60. Sun Tzu, *Art of War*, 152.

CHAPTER 4

1. Sun Tzu, *The Art of War*, 152; Certeau, *The Practice of Everyday Life,* 30. These quotes, from two key definers of "tactics," have popped up throughout.

2. Recently, Levitz and Belkin, "Humanities Fall from Favor,"; Klinkenborg, "The Decline and Fall of the English Major"; Logan, "Poetry: Who Needs It?"

3. I'm thinking more of valuable historical interventions like Elizabeth McHenry's *Forgotten Readers* (2002) or Daniel Kane's *All Poets Welcome: The Lower East Side Poetry Scene in the 1960s* (2003), than the classroom "interpretive communities" popularized by Stanley Fish. The "communities" in McHenry, Kane, and *Texts as Tactics* live in a complex social world, unlike Fish's, which are invariably set in elite, hierarchical classrooms directed by a sage-like professor.

4. This sense certainly aligns with Certeau's "tactic" as a means of resistance in a highly stratified power structure, a "use" that runs contrary to presumptive—or programmatic—uses (30).

5. See Fraser's "Abnormal Justice" in particular.

6. The line, from Auden's "In Memory of W. B. Yeats" (1940), is "poetry makes nothing happen." https://www.poets.org/poetsorg/poem/memory-w-b-yeats.

7. One recent example is Robert Darnton's *Poetry and the Police* (2012), which compellingly traces "six poems through Paris in 1749 as they were declaimed, memorized, reworked, sung, and scribbled on paper amid flurries of other messages, written and oral, during a period of political crisis" (2).

8. Rather than trot out a series of examples, I'll again cite Rita Felski's *Uses of Literature* (2008): "Literary critics love to assign exceptional powers to the texts they read, to write as if the rise of the novel were single-handedly responsible for the formation of bourgeois subjects or to assume that subversive currents of social agitation will flow, as if by fiat, from their favorite piece of performance art" (18).

9. Close reading has been well handled by scholars from across the ideological spectrum. See Lentricchia, *After the New Criticism* (1980); Culler, *Framing the Sign: Criticism and Its Institutions* (1988). As Scholes quips, "Deconstruction is really the New Criticism in fancy dress" (in Bagwell, "An Interview with Robert Scholes," 18).

10. Hayot, *On Literary Worlds,* 17. Hayot may have borrowed his language from *The World, the Text, and the Critic* (1983), in which Edward Said spends some time comparing the New Critical approach to religious mysticism (as opposed to his preferred secular criticism).

11. This is, I would suggest, equally clear in the history of Marxist literary criticism, where the analysis of formal features has often been seen as illuminating a text's political significance. Adorno, to take one example, seems to have decided that literature casts a "spell" largely through his formal reading: "the halo of its uniqueness, its inherent claim to represent something absolute" ("Theses upon Art and Religion Today," 296). A similar formalism underwrites the famous Stalinist dictum about engineering souls. Thus, both sides of the "realism versus the avant-garde" debate within Marxism are marked by the same tendency to read form over use. It's not quite John Crowe Ransom, but it's close.

12. Having apprenticed as a close reader for a decade and a half of my life, I have more to say about Baraka's provocations and the fascinating alignment of statecraft and romance in Shakespeare's sonnet.

13. To name a few, I. A. Richards and Walter Benjamin; Lucien Goldmann and Raymond Williams; Janice Radway and John Frow. And it must be admitted that some of those literary sociologists have relied on close reading, too. The genealogy of reading texts closely to extract large cultural implications runs from Georg Lukács to Lucien Goldmann and even to Bourdieu's *Rules of Art: Genesis and Structure of the Literary Field* (*Les Règles de l'art*, 1992).

14. English, "Everywhere and Nowhere," viii.

15. The field is diverse, as English's quote indicates, but as *Reading as Collective Action* developed, I found myself travelling along two particular—and fairly disparate—paths within that field: systemic analysis, like that produced by Franco Moretti, and the field Robert Darnton, in the mid-1980s, began to call the history of reading. Yet, while sociological approaches have produced new ways of seeing literature's work in the world ("epistemological alterity," in Moretti's useful phrase) they still lacked the fundamental link to everyday politics I was seeking (Moretti, *Distant Reading*, 158). Detailing the political limits (historical, disciplinary) of the sociology of literature is a project for another day.

16. Much of my work in the first chapter draws on the research strategies of the history of reading, pioneered by (among others) Darnton and Chartier; see Chartier's *The Order of Books: Readers, Authors, and Libraries in Europe between the Fourteenth and Eighteenth Centuries* (1994).

17. Hartley and Saltmarsh, "A Brief History of a Movement," 35.

18. Flower, *Community Literacy and the Rhetoric of Public Engagement* (2008), 3.

19. Here are a few examples. Ellison: "In the humanities and in many areas of the arts, collaborative work of any kind is rare, and there is a weak tradition of partnerships by faculty, graduate students, and undergraduates with community and public partners, either individuals or organizations" (113). In a more lamenting tone, "the civic engagement movement needs the humanities, and the humanities need civic engagement. . . . But circumstances, professional pressures, career demands, economic exigencies and institutional inertia, among other frustrations, stand in their way" (Cooper, *Learning in the Plural*, 151–152). As pointed out by service learning guru and literature professor Ed Zlotkowski (mentioned previously), no volume on literature is included in the American Association for Higher Education and Accreditation's twenty-two-volume series on service learning in the disciplines.

20. Ellison, 115.

21. Kevin Bott, in the foreword to *Collaborative Futures: Critical Reflections on Publicly Active Graduate Education* (2012): "I found incredibly talented scholars-in-training, those who wanted to integrate their academic knowledge with their desire to contribute to the public good, living a kind of double existence. They were lying to the advisors whom [*sic*] they knew didn't support public scholarship" (xiv).

22. What to name the field is an important question. As Doberneck et al. point out, the variety of names, from "civically engaged scholars" to "bench to bed-

side," limit the coherence of these approaches and, thus, their potential impact (5–6). Naming things, as I argued with Fraser in the first chapter, matters.

23. E. J. Beckham, in a report for the American Association of Colleges and Universities, writes, "The rhetoric of civic renewal can sound dangerous, threatening to smooth over the gross injustices of the past . . . for America's minority populations" (quoted in Saltmarsh and Hartley, "The Inheritance," 23).

24. Stanley, "Walking a Different Way," 100. Among others, Katharyne Mitchell, introducing the collection *Practising Public Scholarship* (2008), voices a similar lament: "What I do as an academic never seems important enough, or just *enough*" ("Becoming Political," 3).

25. Stanley, 100.

26. "Democratic Engagement," 5, my emphasis. Note the scare quotes on "civic" here, which I think offer another echo of the concerns I described just above.

27. "Integrating Political Activities into Pathways of Engagement," 253.

28. Colby et al., 3.

29. Saltmarsh and Hartley, "The Inheritance of Next-Generation Engagement Scholars," 21.

30. Saltmarsh, Hartley, and Clayton, "Democratic Engagement," 5.

31. Kiesa, "Integrating Political Activities into Pathways of Engagement," 255.

32. Boyte, "The Necessity of Politics," 82.

33. Boyte, *Everyday Politics*, xvii.

34. Bott, Foreword, xxvii.

35. Hengen Fox, "A Habermasian Literary Criticism."

36. See Matthew Specter, *Habermas: An Intellectual Biography*, 31–34.

37. Horkheimer, 216. My emphasis.

38. Ibid., 217, 216.

39. Habermas, *Lifeworld and System*, 372–373.

40. Ibid., 283.

41. Ibid., 355.

42. Ibid., 396–397.

43. Brennan, "Running and Dodging," 280.

44. Laclau and Mouffe, in *Hegemony and Socialist Strategy* (1985), describe identity is the lodestone of political transformation. The full sentence from above: "The

production of this framework, the constitution of the very identities which will have to confront one another antagonistically, becomes now *the first of political problems*" (134, emphasis in original). I agree with their critique of a classical Marxist class analysis: such an approach certainly would not yield insights into the power of the everyday politics I have discussed here. Yet "identity" is not the crucial linking factor in that work, either. Tactical readers did not attempt to reshape *identities*—be they gendered, racialized, classed, whatever—but to reshape *practices*.

45. Hardt and Negri, *Empire*, xi.

46. His focus is most certainly on Western Europe—not surprising given his intellectual heritage and his own national status. But, yes, limited. Despite Habermas's increasing myopic focus on the European project, many have argued his analytic tools go beyond Europe. See Kate Nash's edited collection, including two essays from Nancy Fraser, *Transnationalizing the Public Sphere* (2014).

47. See Tim Brennan, "The Anarchist Sublime," the second section of *Wars of Position*.

48. Habermas, "A Conversation about Questions of Political Theory," 242. Perhaps "European"—given his more recent focus—would be a better adjective.

49. Marx, *Capital*, 125.

50. Habermas, *Reason and the Rationalization of Society*, 285–286.

51. Ibid., 397.

52. While his theory speaks to these concerns broadly, Habermas has also attempted, in various focused essays, to address objections from the poststructuralist to the multiculturalist. With multiculturalists, in particular, he shares a serious interest in questions of inclusion, though approached as questions of the (re)distribution of the rights that grant equal access to well-being. For more on multiculturalism, see the essays that make up *The Inclusion of the Other* (1998).

53. Habermas, *Between Facts and Norms*, 80.

54. Hart, Interview.

55. Habermas, *Lifeworld and System*, 392.

56. I've mentioned Young throughout. For a bit more discussion, see chapter 1.

57. Fraser points out that Habermas's eighteenth-century bourgeois public sphere was also in dialogue with "nationalist publics, popular peasant publics, elite women's publics, and working class publics" ("Rethinking the Public Sphere," 61).

58. Habermas, *Between Facts and Norms*, 360.

59. Ibid., 374.

60. Ibid., 374. My emphasis.

61. Indeed, this word shows up in plenty of writing about engagement; for instance, Steven Yaffee, Julia Wondolleck, and Steven Lippman of the University of Michigan's School of Natural Resources and Environment verb the noun (as I've done here), asking, "What facilitates bridging?" to identify strategies for collaboration among organizations. Not my exact sense, but certainly a parallel case (quoted in Ellison, "The Humanities and the Public Soul," 120).

62. Seen in this light, Boyte's detailed description of everyday politics sounds awfully Habermasian: "negotiations of a pluralist world"; "interacting in order to accomplish some task"; "revitaliz[ing] the public life of institutions" (xi–xii, 4).

63. See Habermas's 1975 *Legitimation Crisis*, for example.

64. Habermas, *Between Facts and Norms*, 374. Again, my emphasis.

65. Habermas offers an elaborate definition of these rights of "citizenship"—a word I'd quibble with, at least in its current understanding—in *Between Facts and Norms*. See, for example, 121–123.

66. I develop this argument in "A Habermasian Literary Criticism," especially on pages 243–249.

67. Longo, Kiesa, Battistoni, "The Future of the Academy with Students as Colleagues," 201.

68. Ibid., 208.

69. Ibid., 208.

70. Saltmarsh et al., "Democratic Engagement," 6.

71. Butin is another next-generation engagement scholar: "community engagement in college may, indeed, have enormous potential to increase. But I would suggest that it will do so not through the traditional models of service learning and civic engagement. It will do so, instead, through the tenacity, vision, and serendipity of individuals finding new, dynamic, and powerful ways to make our education matter to our local and global communities" ("Transformation Is Just Another Word," 250).

72. A 2014 report by the National Student Clearinghouse Research Center suggests that more than 25 percent of students who graduate do so from a different institution than the one where they began college. See Shapiro et al., *Completing College: A State-Level View of Student Attainment Rates*.

73. Both of these concerns are underwritten, as well, by the tenured faculty perspective: the long view, to put it charitably; the view, to take a less charitable tone, of someone with long-term ties to an institution, someone whose career goals may be served by building new structures.

74. In 2009 they made up over 75 percent of faculty members, according to the activist group New Faculty Majority, "Facts about Adjuncts," New Faculty Majority, http://www.newfacultymajority.info/facts-about-adjuncts/.

75. According to Kiesa, "It ought to be a red flag that college students' engagement is so much higher than noncollege youth engagement and that even on a highly engaged and well-resourced campus like Tufts, the politically engaged students are the most advantaged" ("Integrating Political Activities into Pathways of Engagement," 257).

76. One recent example is the case of Steven Salaita, a tenured faculty member whose tweets about Israeli settlements in Palestinian territory led to him losing a job that he had been offered (and left him, for a time, jobless). His own account, "Why I Was Fired," includes the key details.

77. This idea of networking across institutions is a key piece of M. V. Lee Badgett's *The Public Professor: How to Use Your Research to Change the World* (2016): "Build a network of relationships that extends into the work and institutions you hope to influence" (13).

EPILOGUE

1. E-mail me, please: nicholashengen@gmail.com.

2. Aubry, *Reading as Therapy: What Contemporary Fiction Does for Middle-Class Americans.*

3. Banks, *Continental Drift*, 410.

Bibliography

Adorno, Theodor W. "Theses upon Art and Religion Today." In *Notes to Literature*, vol. 2, edited by Rolf Tiedemann and translated by Shierry Weber Nicholsen, 292–298. New York: Columbia University Press, 1992.

Amichai, Yehuda. *The Selected Poetry of Yehuda Amichai*. Edited and translated by Chana Bloch and Stephen Mitchell. New York: Harper and Row, 1986.

"Arguments through the Ages; W. H. Auden: The 'odour of death / Offends the September night.'" *Minneapolis Star Tribune*, October 15, 2001, 11A.

Aubry, Timothy. *Reading as Therapy: What Contemporary Fiction Does for Middle-Class Americans*. Iowa City: University of Iowa Press, 2011.

Auden, W. H. "September 1, 1939." In *The Norton Anthology of Modern and Contemporary Poetry*, edited by Jahan Ramazani, 801–803. New York: Norton, 2003.

Badgett, M. V. Lee. *The Public Professor: How to Use Your Research to Change the World*. New York: New York University Press, 2016.

Bagwell, J. Timothy. "An Interview with Robert Scholes." *Iowa Journal of Literary Studies* 4.2 (1983): 13–20.

Baker, Sara. Interview with author, June 8, 2009.

Banks, Russell. *Continental Drift*. New York: Harper, 1985.

Baraka, Amiri. *Black Magic: Sabotage, Target Study, Black Art: Collected Poetry, 1961–1967*. Indianapolis, IN.: Bobbs-Merrill, 1969.

———. "Confessions of a Former Anti-Semite." *Village Voice*, December 17, 1980, 1, 19–23.

———. *Somebody Blew Up America & Other Poems*. Philipsburg, GP (St. Martin): House of Nehesi, 2003.

Benson, Jackson J. "'To Tom, Who Lived It': John Steinbeck and the Man from Weedpatch." *Journal of Modern Literature* 5.2 (1976): 151–210.

Bernstein, Richard. "Poetry's Insights on Pain and Joy." *New York Times*, September 13, 2001, E1.

BET Tonight. "America on Alert: Why Is America Hated?" *BET Tonight.* October 10, 2001.

Bikerts, Sven. "Disaster Calls Poetry to Action; Auden's Verses Are Back at Work." *New York Observer,* October 1, 2001, 1.

Billeaudeaux, Andre, David Domke, John S. Hutcheson, and Philip Garland. "Newspaper Editorials Follow Lead of Bush Administration." In *Media in an American Crisis: Studies of September 11, 2001,* edited by Elinor Kelley Grusin and Sandra H. Utt, 61–76. Lanham, MD: University Press of America, 2005.

Blouin, David D., and Evelyn M. Perry. "Whom Does Service Learning Really Serve? Community-Based Organizations' Perspectives on Service Learning." *Teaching Sociology* 37.2 (2009): 120–135.

Bott, Kevin. Foreword. In *Collaborative Futures: Critical Reflections on Publicly Active Graduate Education,* edited by Amanda Gilvin, Georgia M. Roberts, and Craig Martin, xxi–xxvi. Syracuse, NY: Graduate School Press of Syracuse University, 2012.

Bourdieu, Pierre. *Distinction: A Social Critique of the Judgement of Taste.* Translated by Richard Nice. Cambridge, MA: Harvard University Press, 1984.

———. *The Rules of Art: Genesis and Structure of the Literary Field.* Translated by Susan Emanuel. Stanford, CA: Stanford University Press, 1995.

Boyte, Harry C. *Everyday Politics: Reconnecting Citizens and Public Life.* Philadelphia: University of Pennsylvania Press, 2004.

———. "The Necessity of Politics." *Journal of Public Affairs* 7.1 (2004): 75–85.

Brennan, Timothy. "Running and Dodging: The Rhetoric of Doubleness in Contemporary Theory." *New Literary History* 41.2 (2010): 277–299.

———. *Wars of Position: The Cultural Politics of Left and Right.* New York: Columbia University Press, 2006.

Burt, Stephen. "'September 1, 1939' Revisited: Or, Poetry, Politics, and the Idea of the Public." *American Literary History* 15.3 (2003): 533–559.

Bush, George W. "Freedom at War with Fear: Address to a Joint Session of Congress and the American People." Speech, US Congress, Washington, DC, September 20, 2001. Accessed 4 April 2007. http://usatoday30.usatoday.com/news/nation/2001/09/21/bush-text.htm.

Bushouse, Brenda. "Community Nonprofit Organizations and Service Learning: Resource Constraints to Building Partnerships with Universities." *Michigan Journal of Community Service Learning* 12.1 (2005): 32–40.

Butin, Dan W. "Transformation Is Just Another Word: Thinking through the Future of Community Engagement in the Disrupted University." In *Deepening Community Engagement in Higher Education: Forging New Pathways,* edited by

Ariane Hoy and Mathew Johnson, 245–252. New York: Palgrave Macmillan, 2013.

Butler, Judith. *Precarious Life: The Powers of Mourning and Violence.* New York: Verso, 2006.

Campus Compact. *Creating a Culture of Assessment: 2012 Annual Member Survey.* Boston: Campus Compact, 2012.

Carler, Donna. Interview with Author, June 3, 2009.

Carter, Bill, and Felicity Barringer. "In Patriotic Time, Dissent Is Muted." *New York Times*, September 28, 2001, 1.

Casanova, Pascale. *The World Republic of Letters*. Translated by M. B. Debevoise. Cambridge, MA: Harvard University Press, 2005.

Cash, Angela. Interview with Author, June 10, 2009.

Certeau, Michel de. *The Practice of Everyday Life*. Translated by Steven Rendall. Berkeley: University of California Press, 1984.

Cervantes, Lorna Dee. "Palestine." *About.com: Poems after the Attack*, Accessed 2 October 2010.

Chang, Nancy. *Silencing Political Dissent: How Post-September 11 Anti-Terrorism Measures Threaten Our Civil Liberties.* New York: Seven Stories Press, 2002.

Chartier, Roger. *The Order of Books: Readers, Authors, and Libraries in Europe between the Fourteenth and Eighteenth Centuries.* Translated by Lydia G. Cochrane. London: Polity Press, 1994.

"City of Bridgeport and National Endowment for the Arts Host Mrs. Laura Bush for Big Read Celebration." Press release, April 16, 2007. Washington, DC: National Endowment for the Arts. Accessed 8 August 2009.

Claibourne, Mary Pom. Interview with Author, June 10, 2009.

Colby, Anne, E. Beaumont, Thomas Ehrlich, and Josh Corngold. *Educating for Democracy: Preparing Undergraduates for Responsible Political Engagement.* San Francisco: Jossey-Bass, 2007.

Collier, Michael. "A Poem from September 1939 Reaches Out to September 2001." *Baltimore Sun*, September 16, 2001, F3.

Cooper, David D. *Learning in the Plural: Essays on the Humanities in Public Life.* East Lansing: Michigan State University, 2014.

Crandall, Samantha. Interview with Author, June 9, 2009.

Culler, Jonathan. *Framing the Sign: Criticism and Its Institutions.* Norman: University of Oklahoma Press, 1988.

Cummings, Claire. "Big Read Book Strikes a Chord with Jackson Residents." *Jackson Citizen Patriot*, March 1, 2009, A5.

D'Arlach, Lucia, Bernadette Sánchez, and Rachel Feuer. "Voices from the Community: A Case for Reciprocity in Service Learning." *Michigan Journal of Community Service Learning* 16.1 (2009): 5–16.

Darnton, Robert. *Poetry and the Police: Communication Networks in Eighteenth-Century Paris*. Cambridge, MA: Belknap Press of Harvard University Press, 2010.

Doberneck, Diane M., Chris R. Glass, and John Schweitzer. "From Rhetoric to Reality: A Typology of Publicly Engaged Scholarship." *Journal of Higher Education Outreach and Engagement* 14.4 (2010): 5–35.

Dry, Rachel. "John Steinbeck Would Love This Recession." *Washington Post*, March 22, 2009. Accessed 9 April 2011. http://www.washingtonpost.com/wp-dyn/content/article/2009/03/20/AR2009032001778.html.

Ellison, Julie. "The Humanities and the Public Soul." In *Practising Public Scholarship: Experiences and Possibilities beyond the Academy*, edited by Katharyne Mitchell, 113–121. Chichester, UK: Wiley-Blackwell, 2008.

English, James F. "Everywhere and Nowhere: The Sociology of Literature after 'the Sociology of Literature.'" *New Literary History* 41.2 (2010): v–xxiii.

Feldman, Leonard C. "Redistribution, Recognition, and the State: The Irreducibly Political Dimension of Injustice." *Political Theory* 30.3 (2002): 410–440.

Felski, Rita. *Uses of Literature*. Malden, MA: Blackwell, 2008.

Fish, Stanley. *Is There a Text in This Class? The Authority of Interpretive Communities*. Cambridge, MA: Harvard University Press, 1980.

Fitzgerald, H. E., K. Bruns, S. Sonka, A. Furco, L. Swanson. "The Centrality of Engagement in Higher Education." *Journal of Higher Education Outreach and Engagement* 16.3 (2012): 7–28.

Flower, Linda. *Community Literacy and the Rhetoric of Public Engagement*. Carbondale: Southern Illinois University Press, 2008.

Fowler, Alastair. *Kinds of Literature: An Introduction to the Theory of Genres and Modes*. Cambridge, MA: Harvard University Press, 1982.

Fraser, Nancy. "Abnormal Justice." *Critical Inquiry* 34.3 (2008): 393–422.

———. "Reframing Justice in a Globalizing World." *New Left Review* 36 (2005): 69–88.

———. "Rethinking the Public Sphere: A Contribution to the Critique of Actually Existing Democracy." *Social Text* 25/26 (1990): 56–80.

Fraser, Nancy, and Axel Honneth. *Redistribution or Recognition?: A Political-Philosophical Exchange*. New York: Verso, 2003.

Freire, Paolo. *Pedagogy of the Oppressed: New Revised 20th-Anniversary Edition*. Translated by Myra Bergman Ramos. New York: Continuum, 1993.

Ginsberg, Allen. *Collected Poems: 1947–1997*. New York: Harper, 2006.

Gioia, Dana. "Prepared Statement of Dana Gioia, Chairman of the National Endowment for the Arts," Appropriations Subcommittee on Interior, Environment, and Related Agencies US House of Representatives, April 1, 2008, Washington, DC. Accessed 29 September 2009.

Giroux, Henry A. *Impure Acts: The Practical Politics of Cultural Studies*. New York: Routledge, 2000.

Graeber, David. *Debt: The First 5,000 Years*. New York: Melville House, 2011.

Griffin, Walter. "At Belfast Library, Residents Mark Month of Mourning." *Bangor Daily News*, October 12, 2001, 1.

Grobman, Laurie. "Is There a Place for Service Learning in Literary Studies?" *Profession* (2005): 129–140.

Guerrieri, Kevin. "*Leer y escribir la frontera*: Language, Literature, and Community Engagement in the San Diego–Tijuana Borderlands." In *Community-Based Learning and the Work of Literature*, edited by Susan Danielson and Ann Marie Fallon, 154–179. Bolton, MA: Anker, 2007.

Guillory, John. *Cultural Capital: The Problem of Literary Canon Formation*. Chicago: University of Chicago Press, 1993.

Gutmann, Amy. Introduction. In *Multiculturalism: Examining the Politics of Recognition*, edited by Amy Gutmann, 3–24. Princeton, NJ: Princeton University Press, 1994.

Gwiazda, Piotr. "The Aesthetics of Politics / The Politics of Aesthetics: Amiri Baraka's 'Somebody Blew Up America.'" *Contemporary Literature* 45.3 (2004): 460–485.

Habermas, Jürgen. *Between Facts and Norms: Contributions to a Discourse Theory of Law and Democracy*. Translated by William Rehg. Cambridge, MA: MIT Press, 1996.

———. "A Conversation about Questions of Political Theory." In *Discourse and Democracy: Essays on Habermas's "Between Facts and Norms,"* edited by René von Schomberg and Kenneth Baynes, 241–258. Albany: State University of New York Press, 2002.

———. *The Inclusion of the Other: Studies in Political Theory*. Edited by Ciaran Cronin and Pablo De Greiff. Translated by Ciaran Cronin. Cambridge, MA: MIT University Press, 1998.

———. *Legitimation Crisis*. Translated by Thomas McCarthy. Boston: Beacon Press, 1975.

———. *Lifeworld and System: A Critique of Functionalist Reason*. Vol. 2 of *The Theory of Communicative Action*. Translated by Thomas McCarthy. Boston: Beacon Press, 1987.

———. *The Philosophical Discourse of Modernity: Twelve Lectures*. Translated by Frederick G. Lawrence. Cambridge, MA: MIT Press, 1987.

———. *Reason and the Rationalization of Society*. Vol. 1 of *The Theory of Communicative Action*. Translated by Thomas McCarthy. Boston: Beacon Press, 1984.

Hamod, Sam. "After the Funeral of Assam Hamady." In *Unsettling America: An Anthology of Contemporary Multicultural Poetry*, edited by Maria Mazziotti Gillan and Jennifer Gillan, 288–291. New York: Penguin, 1994.

Hardt, Michael, and Antonio Negri. *Empire*. Cambridge, MA: Harvard University Press, 2000.

Hart, Jon, Interview with Author, June 3, 2009.

Hartley, Matthew, and John Saltmarsh. "A Brief History of a Movement: Civic Engagement and American Higher Education." In *Publicly Engaged Scholars: Next-Generation Engagement and the Future of Higher Education*, edited by Margaret A. Post, Elaine Ward, Nicholas V. Longo, and John Saltmarsh, 34–60. Sterling, VA: Stylus, 2016.

Harty, John. *James Joyce's "Finnegans Wake": A Casebook*. New York: Garland, 1991.

Hayot, Eric. *On Literary Worlds*. New York: Oxford University Press, 2012.

Heaney, Seamus. *The Cure at Troy: A Version of Sophocles' Philoctetes*. London: Faber and Faber, 1990.

Hengen Fox, Nicholas. "A Habermasian Literary Criticism." *New Literary History* 43.2 (Spring 2012): 235–254.

———. "Poetry, Recognition, and Redistribution: The September 11 Chronocanon." *American Literature* 87.1 (2015): 159–186.

———. "Teaching (Is Not) Activism." *Radical Teacher* 94 (2012): 14–23.

Henkin, David. *City Reading: Written Words and Public Spaces in Antebellum New York*. New York: Columbia University Press, 1998.

Henry, Sue Ellen. "'I Can Never Turn My Back On That': Liminality and the Impact of Class on Service-Learning Experience." In *Looking In, Teaching Out: Critical Issues and Directions in Service-Learning*, edited by Dan Butin, 45–66. New York: Palgrave Press, 2005.

Horkheimer, Max. *Critical Theory: Selected Essays*. Translated by Matthew J. O'Connell and others. New York: Continuum, 1986.

Howie, Linsey M. "Speaking Subjects: A Reading of Women's Book Groups." PhD diss., Latrobe University, 1998.

Iser, Wolfgang. "The Reading Process: A Phenomenological Approach." In *Reader-Response Criticism: From Formalism to Post-Structuralism*, edited by Jane P. Tompkins, 50–69. Baltimore, MD: Johns Hopkins University Press, 1980.

Johnson, Dennis Loy, and Valerie Merians. *Poetry after 9/11: An Anthology of New York Poets*. Hoboken, NJ: Melville House, 2002.

Kakutani, Michiko. "Rituals for Grieving Extend Past Tradition into Public Displays." *New York Times*, September 18, 2011, B11.

Kane, Daniel. *All Poets Welcome: The Lower East Side Poetry Scene in the 1960s.* Berkeley: University of California Press, 2003.

Kiesa, Abby. "Integrating Political Activities into Pathways of Engagement." In *Deepening Community Engagement in Higher Education: Forging New Pathways,* edited by Ariane Hoy and Mathew Johnson. New York: Palgrave Macmillan, 2013.

Kemp-Welch, A. *Stalin and the Literary Intelligentsia, 1928–39.* London: Macmillan, 1991.

Klinkenborg, Verlyn. "The Decline and Fall of the English Major." *New York Times,* June 22, 2013, SR10.

Laclau, Ernesto, and Chantal Mouffe. *Hegemony and Socialist Strategy: Toward a Radical Democratic Politics.* London: Verso, 2001.

Lambert Lee, Kate. *Faces of Poverty.* Community Action Agency. Jackson, MI, 2009.

———. Interview with Author, June 5, 2009.

Landrum, Cynthia. "Grapes of Wrath." Sermon. Unitarian Universalist Church of East Liberty, Jackson, MI. March 15, 2009.

———. Interview with Author, June 2, 2009.

———. "Our Ministry in Difficult Times." Sermon. Unitarian Universalist Church of East Liberty, Jackson, MI. March 22, 2009.

Leadership Conference on Civil Rights. "Wrong Then, Wrong Now: Racial Profiling before & after September 11, 2001." Washington, DC: Leadership Conference on Civil Rights Education Fund, 2003.

Lecercle, Jean-Jacques. "Return to the Political." *PMLA* 125.4 (2010): 916–919.

Lentricchia, Frank. *After the New Criticism.* Chicago: University of Chicago Press, 1981.

Levitz, Jennifer, and Douglas Belkin. "Humanities Fall from Favor." *Wall Street Journal,* June 6, 2013.

Logan, William. "Poetry: Who Needs It?" *New York Times,* June 14, 2014, SR 5.

Long, Elizabeth. *Book Clubs: Women and the Uses of Reading in Everyday Life.* Chicago: University of Chicago Press, 2003.

Longo, Nicholas V., Abby Kiesa, and Richard Battistoni, "The Future of the Academy with Students as Colleagues." In *Publicly Engaged Scholars: Next-Generation Engagement and the Future of Higher Education,* edited by Margaret A. Post, Elaine Ward, Nicholas V. Longo, and John Saltmarsh, 197–213. Sterling, VA: Stylus, 2016.

Marx, Karl. *Capital, Volume I.* Translated by Ben Fowkes. New York: Penguin, 1990.

———. "The Eighteenth Brumaire of Louis Bonaparte." In *Later Political Writings,* edited and translated by Terrell Carver, 31–127. Cambridge: Cambridge University Press, 1996.

Massing, Michael. "Press Watch." In *A Just Response:* The Nation *on Terrorism, Democracy, and September 11*, edited by Katrina vanden Heuvel, 185–208. New York: Nation Books, 2002.

McHenry, Elizabeth. *Forgotten Readers: Recovering the Lost History of African American Literary Societies*. Durham, NC: Duke University Press, 2002.

McHenry, Eric. "Auden on Bin Laden." *Slate*, September 20, 2001. Accessed 25 March 2009. http://www.slate.com/articles/arts/culturebox/2001/09/auden_on_bin_laden.html.

Mearsheimer, John J., and Stephen M. Walt. *The Israel Lobby and U.S. Foreign Policy*. New York: Farrar, Straus and Giroux, 2008.

Mendelson, Edward. *Later Auden*. London: Faber and Faber, 1999.

Miles, Kathryn. "Get Up, Stand Up: Teaching Civil Disobedience in the Literature Classroom." *PMLA* 124.3 (2009): 864–869.

Millard, Bonnie. Interview with Author, June 9, 2009.

Mitchell, Katharyne. "Becoming Political." In *Practising Public Scholarship: Experiences and Possibilities beyond the Academy*, edited by Katharyne Mitchell, 1–5. Chichester, UK: Wiley-Blackwell, 2008.

Mitchell, Tania D. "Traditional vs. Critical Service-Learning: Engaging the Literature to Differentiate Two Models." *Michigan Journal of Community Service Learning* 14.2 (2008): 50–65.

Molesworth, Charles. *Marianne Moore: A Literary Life*. New York: Atheneum, 1990.

Mollis, Kara L. "Servicing Reading: Community Work and the Revaluation of Literary Study." In *Community-Based Learning and the Work of Literature*, edited by Susan Danielson and Ann Marie Fallon, 46–62. Bolton, MA: Anker, 2007.

Moore, Marianne. *The Complete Poems of Marianne Moore*. New York: MacMillan, 1967.

Moretti, Franco. *Distant Reading*. London: Verso, 2013.

Morton, Keith. "The Irony of Service: Charity, Project, and Social Change in Service-Learning." *Michigan Journal of Community Service Learning* 2.1 (1995): 19–32.

Nash, Kate. *Transnationalizing the Public Sphere*. Cambridge, UK: Polity, 2014.

"National Endowment for the Arts Announces More Than $1.5 Million in Big Read Grants for First Half of 2008." Press release, November 13, 2007. Washington, DC: National Endowment for the Arts. Accessed 2 August 2009.

"National Endowment for the Arts Announces The Big Read." Press release,

December 20, 2005. Washington, DC: National Endowment for the Arts. Accessed 17 July 2009.

NewsHour with Jim Lehrer. PBS. September 18, 2001.

Nguyen, Tram. *We Are All Suspects Now: Untold Stories from Immigrant Communities after 9/11.* Boston: Beacon Press, 2005.

Oliveri, Jackie. "Emotions Are Shared in Library Gatherings." *Portland Press Herald,* October 12, 2001, A4.

"Open Letter from the Metropolitan Museum of Art." *New York Times* (advertisement), September 21, 2001, E28.

Parini, Jay. *John Steinbeck: A Biography.* London: Heinemann, 1994.

Petrucci, Armando. "Reading to Read: A Future for Reading." In *A History of Reading in the West,* edited by Guglielmo Cavallo and Roger Chartier and translated by Lydia G. Cochrane, 345–367. Amherst: University of Massachusetts Press, 2003.

"Poet Sam Hamod Reads One of His Poems." *Weekend Edition Saturday.* National Public Radio. September 29, 2001.

Poncavage, Joanna. "When People Turn to Poetry; The Power to Tame Terror." *Allentown Morning Call,* September 23, 2001, E1.

Post, Margaret A., Elaine Ward, Nicholas V. Longo, and John Saltmarsh, eds. *Publicly Engaged Scholars: Next-Generation Engagement and the Future of Higher Education.* Sterling, VA: Stylus, 2016.

Price, John. "The New American War: True Patriotism or Blind Loyalty?" *New York Amsterdam News,* September 27, 2001, 1.

Putnam, Robert D. *Bowling Alone: The Collapse and Revival of American Community.* New York: Simon and Schuster, 2001.

Ragsdale, Mike. Interview with Author, June 13, 2009.

Ramazani, Jahan. "Writing Life: Remaking a Norton Anthology." *VQR* 80.2 (2004). Accessed 10 September 2015. http://www.vqronline.org/essay/writing-life-remaking-norton-anthology.

Reading at Risk: A Survey of Literary Reading in America. Washington, DC: National Endowment for the Arts, 2004.

Rhoads, Robert A. *Freedom's Web: Student Activism in the Age of Cultural Diversity.* Baltimore, MD: Johns Hopkins University Press, 2000.

Rich, Adrienne. *Dark Fields of the Republic: Poems 1991–1995.* New York: W. W. Norton, 1995.

Ruhe, Pierre. "A Dose of Painting, Poetry, and Music in Troubled Times." *Atlanta Journal-Constitution,* September 23, 2001, E12.

Rukeyser, Muriel. *The Collected Poems of Muriel Rukeyser.* Pittsburgh, PA: University of Pittsburgh Press, 2005.

Said, Edward W. *The World, the Text, and the Critic*. Cambridge, MA: Harvard University Press, 1983.

Salaita, Steven. "Why I Was Fired." *Chronicle of Higher Education*, October 5, 2015.

Saltmarsh, John, and Matt Hartley. "The Inheritance of Next-Generation Engagement Scholars." In *Publicly Engaged Scholars: Next-Generation Engagement and the Future of Higher Education*, edited by Margaret A. Post, Elaine Ward, Nicholas V. Longo, and John Saltmarsh, 15–33. Sterling, VA: Stylus, 2016.

Saltmarsh, John, Matt Hartley, and Patti Clayton. "Democratic Engagement White Paper." Boston: New England Resource Center for Higher Education, 2009.

Sarah, Robyn. "Poetry Has Words for Times Like These." *Montreal Gazette*, October 13, 2001, J5.

Sayles, Amy. Interview with Author, June 3, 2009.

Schmich, Mary. "Poetry Soothes the Soul in These Painful Days." *Chicago Tribune*, September 23, 2001, 4C.

Schultz, Susan M. *A Poetics of Impasse in Modern and Contemporary American Poetry*. Tuscaloosa: University of Alabama Press, 2005.

Shakespeare, William. *The Sonnets: Updated Edition.* Edited by G. Blakemore Evans. Cambridge: Cambridge University Press, 2006.

Shapiro, D., A. Dundar, P. K. Wakhungu, X. Yuan, and A. T. Harrell. *Completing College: A State-Level View of Student Attainment Rates* (Signature Report No. 6a). Herndon, VA: National Student Clearinghouse Research Center, 2014.

Sheffield, Eric C. "Service Learning as a Democratic, Public Affair." *Journal of Public Affairs* 7.1 (2004): 1–15.

Shelley, Percy. *Shelley's Poetry and Prose.* Edited by Donald H. Reiman and Sharon B. Powers. New York: Norton, 1977.

Smith, Dinitia. "In Shelley or Auden, in the Sonnet or Free Verse, the Eerily Intimate Power of Poetry to Console." *New York Times*, October 1, 2001, E1.

Smith, Stephen. "Seeking Solace in the Words." *Record* (Bergen County, NJ), October 14, 2001, F01.

Specter, Matthew G. *Habermas: An Intellectual Biography*. Cambridge: Cambridge University Press, 2010.

Stanley, Talmage A. "'Walking a Different Way': Coeducators, Co-learners, and Democratic Engagement Renaming the World." In *Deepening Community Engagement in Higher Education: Forging New Pathways*, edited by Ariane Hoy and Mathew Johnson, 95–104. New York: Palgrave Macmillan, 2013.

Steinbeck, John. *The Grapes of Wrath*. New York: Penguin, 1999.

———. "The Harvest Gypsies." In *The Grapes of Wrath and Other Writings: 1936–1941*, 991–1022. New York: Library of America, 1996.

Sun Tzu. *The Art of War: The New Illustrated Edition*. Translated by Samuel B. Griffith. London: Watkins, 2005.
Sutherland, John. "The Ideas Interview: Franco Moretti." *Guardian* (UK), January 9, 2006.
Szink, Judy. Interview with Author, June 1, 2009.
Taylor, Charles. "The Politics of Recognition." In *Multiculturalism: Examining the Politics of Recognition*, edited by Amy Gutmann, 25–74. Princeton, NJ: Princeton University Press, 1994.
Teres, Harvey. *The Word on the Street: Linking the Academy and the Common Reader*. Ann Arbor: University of Michigan Press, 2010.
Thaler, Richard H., and Cass Sunstein. *Nudge: Improving Decisions about Health, Wealth, and Happiness*. New York: Penguin, 2008.
"To Our Readers." *Morning Call* (Allentown, PA), September 18, 2001, A18.
Toner, Robin. "Civil Liberty vs. Security: Finding a Wartime Balance." *New York Times*, November 18, 2001.
Trebay, Guy. "At a Loss and Craving Order." *New York Times*, September 23, 2001, ST1.
Velasquez, Loida. Interview with Author, June 8, 2009.
Verhovek, Sam Howe. "Americans Give In to Race Profiling." *New York Times*, September 23, 2001, A1.
Volk, Jane. Interview with Author, June 3, 2009.
von Hallberg, Robert. *Lyric Powers*. Chicago: University of Chicago Press, 2008.
Wartzman, Rick. *Obscene in the Extreme: The Burning and Banning of John Steinbeck's "The Grapes of Wrath"*. New York: PublicAffairs, 2008.
Welch, Michael. *Scapegoats of September 11: Hate Crimes and State Crimes in the War on Terror*. New Brunswick, NJ: Rutgers University Press, 2006.
Williams, Raymond. *The Long Revolution*. New York: Columbia University Press, 1961.
Young, Iris Marion. "Communication and the Other: Beyond Deliberative Democracy." In *Democracy and Difference: Contesting the Boundaries of the Political*, edited by Seyla Benhabib, 120–135. Princeton, NJ: Princeton University Press, 1996.
———. *Inclusion and Democracy*. New York: Oxford University Press, 2000.
Zagajewski, Adam. "Try to Praise the Mutilated World." *New Yorker*, September 24, 2001, 96.
Zlotkowski, Edward. Introduction. In *Community-Based Learning and the Work of Literature*, edited by Susan Danielson and Ann Marie Fallon, xii. Bolton, MA: Anker, 2007.

Index

Adorno, Theodor, 33, 93, 95
anthology (alternative definitions), 9–25, 30
Auden, W. H., 10–12, 14, 24, 29, 31, 86, 97

Banks, Russell, 110
Baraka, Amiri, 9, 12, 17, 22–27, 31, 80
Big Read, the, 4, 36–40, 43–50, 55–59, 85, 96–99
book clubs, 36, 38, 45–59
Book Clubs (Elizabeth Long), 48–49
Bourdieu, Pierre, 12, 68
Boyte, Harry, 2, 75, 91, 100–103
Bush, George W., 8, 15–16, 25, 28

canon (definition), 12–13, 16, 26, 32–33, 85–86
Cervantes, Lorna Dee, 3, 9–10, 16, 19–24, 32
civic engagement: critique, 89–91. *See also* service learning
close reading, 66, 87–89, 109
community (definition), 41, 44–53, 58, 85–86, 98, 113
critical service learning. *See also* service learning

Frankfurt School, 69, 88, 93, 95
Fraser, Nancy: critique of public sphere, 30, 98–99. *See also* recognition; redistribution; representation
Freire, Paolo, 70, 73, 96, 103

Giroux, Henry, 91, 96
Grapes of Wrath (Steinbeck), 35–36, 39–44, 50–52, 56, 57, 59

Habermas, Jürgen: and the Frankfurt School, 92–96; public sphere criticism, 98–99; radical education theory, 96; *Theory of Communicative Action*, 6–7, 87, 96–103
Hamod, Sam, 9, 11, 17–19, 21, 24–25
Hardt, Michael and Antonio Negri, 95
Horkheimer, Max, 93–95
Huntington, Samuel, 8

justice (definition), 2–3. *See also* recognition; redistribution; representation

Lange, Dorothea, 38–39, 71–72, 98
literature: as dead, 84, 108, 119; as elitist, 38, 109; learning to read, 62; as mediator, 76; as political, 87, 91

Marx, Karl: *Capital*, 96; *Eighteenth Brumaire of Louis Bonaparte*, 25, 32, 57, 64, 66; and the Frankfurt School, 93–97

Mouffe, Chantal and Ernesto Laclau, 95

National Endowment for the Arts, 36–38, 84
National Public Radio, 11, 13, 18, 19, 29, 37, 59, 83, 106
New Criticism, 98. *See also* close reading
New Sociology of Literature, 88

politics: absence from literary criticism, 87–89, 91–92, 94–95; definition, 2–3, 91. *See also* recognition; redistribution; representation
Political Engagement Project, 78–79, 82, 90
public engagement. *See also* civic engagement; service learning
public sphere, 30, 98–99

reading groups. *See also* book clubs
recognition, 2, 4, 9–10, 16–17, 31–35, 50, 53, 57, 59, 63, 72, 74, 76, 83, 86–87, 91, 107
redistribution, 4, 10, 26, 31–35, 41, 44, 50, 52, 59, 63, 70, 74, 83, 91, 103
representation, 2–4, 9–10, 31, 33, 35, 57, 63, 67, 74, 83, 86, 87, 100, 103, 107; literary vs. political, 25–26, 32
research methods for this book, 5, 33, 36, 62–63

September 11, 2001, 8–10; media responses, 18–19
service learning, 16, 50, 63, 74–82, 100, 104; as apolitical, 88–90; critical service-learning distinction, 75–76

tactics (definition), 2–3, 5, 57–58, 60, 80, 82, 84–87

Young, Iris Marion, 24–25, 80, 98

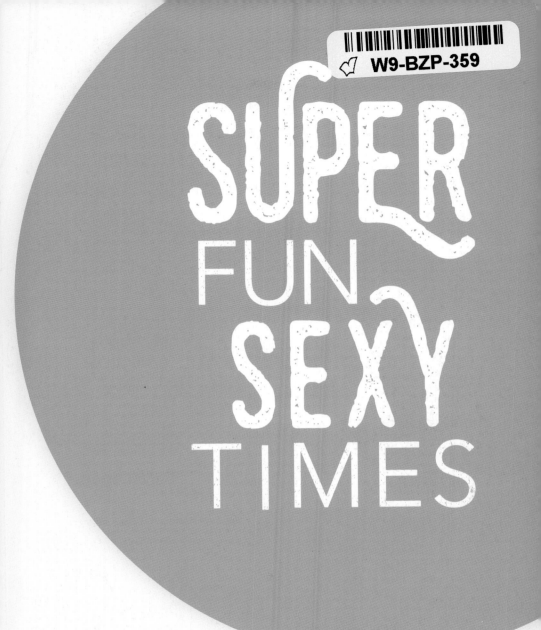

SUPER FUN SEXY TIMES

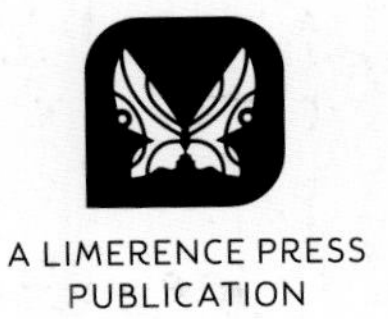

A LIMERENCE PRESS
PUBLICATION

SUPER FUN SEXY TIMES

BY MEREDITH MCCLAREN

Many thanks to my patient beta readers for their guidance.

Designed by Kate Z. Stone
Edited by Ari Yarwood

Published by Limerence Press
Ari Yarwood, founder & editorial director

limerencepress.com
@limerencepress

meredithmcclaren.tumblr.com
@IniquitousFish

1319 SE Martin Luther King, Jr. Blvd.
Suite 240
Portland, OR 97214

First Edition: August 2019
ISBN: 978-1-62010-650-1
eISBN: 978-1-62010-651-8

10 9 8 7 6 5 4 3 2 1

Library of Congress Control Number:
2019931599

Printed in Hong Kong.

Thank you for buying this book so my baby can afford dental insurance.

—MEREDITH'S MOM

CHAPTER 1

WORST CASE SCENARIO

So here we are—
Nope. No talking while I'm thinking.

Nope.
Stop.

I didn't say anything.
Do you know how to get out of here?
No.
Then you have nothing to say. Now let me think.

This isn't so bad, Wonder.

Which part? The being trapped in an enclosed space? The being trapped in an enclosed space AND being rival sidekicks—
No, no. You're the sidekick. I'm a mercenary. I have enough sense to get paid for getting the mickey knocked out of me.

How about... I'm in an enclosed space and you're stunningly attractive?

I am that, Jack.
But try harder.

Your boss will find us? That's a plus, right? I mean, I'm just hired help. My ice hands are a bonus, but my dude can buy a dozen of me. He's not looking.
...
That might be... overly generous.

I mean, he WILL find us. But it could be a while. He gets... distracted.
Hm. True.

Chemicals!
Chemicals?
So there. It's not as bad as it could have been.
We just had a fight.
In a "mad" scientist's underground, enclosed, under-circulated laboratory.
Where there are BOTTLES. Full of CHEMICALS. And we seem to have broken half of them.

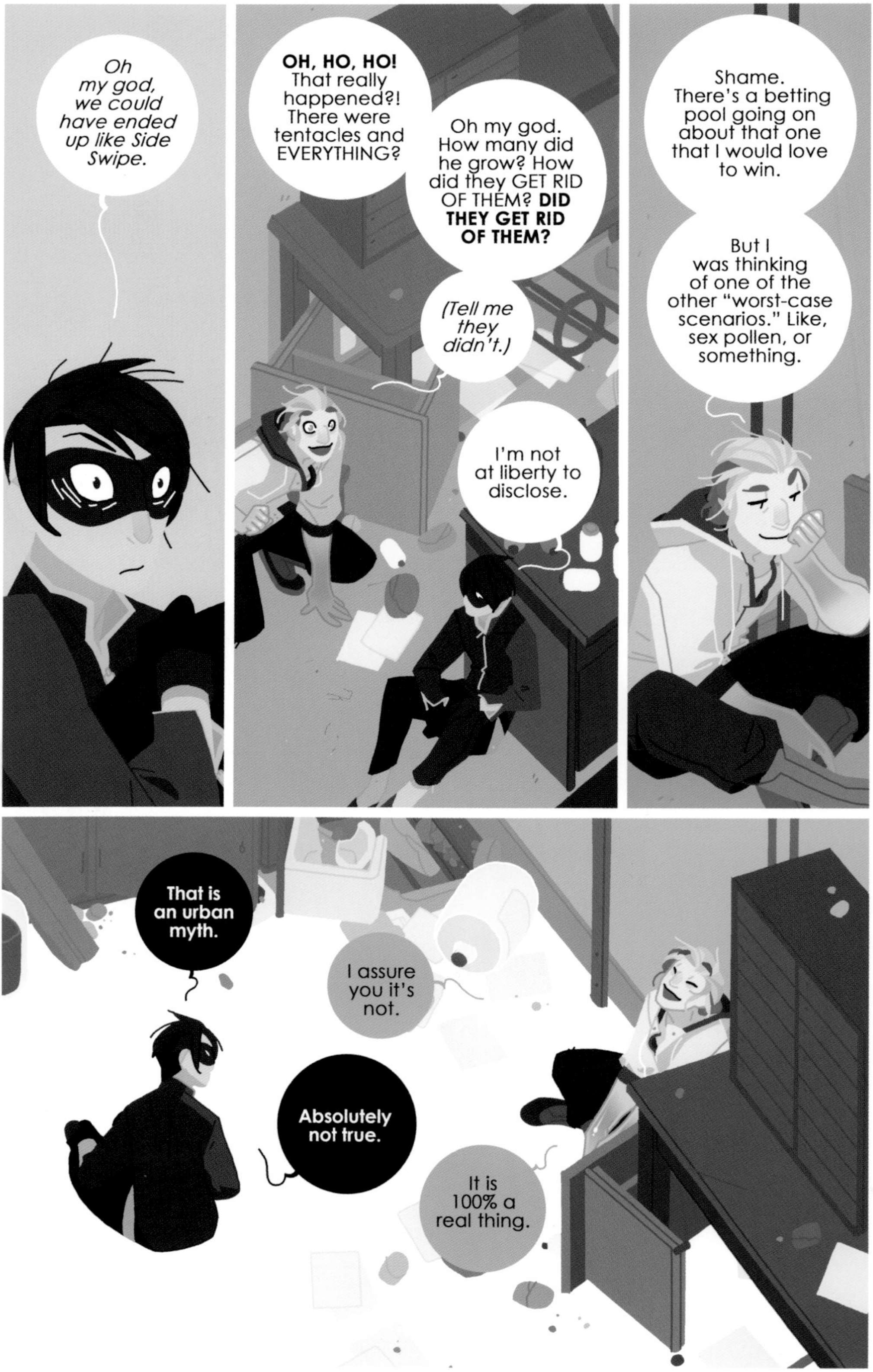

That is an urban myth.

I assure you it's not.

Absolutely not true.

It is 100% a real thing.

We've had some doozies.

Did anyone DIE?

Good lord, no. Bull Shark had blood diverted a little too long during one round of testing, though. He needed a bit of time to recover from that.

WHY would you SAY that? Now I have an image of Bull Shark with an erection stuck in my head.

He's part shark.

What?

He's part shark.

...I will never be able to un-know that....
...
You're kinda really miserable, huh?
Little bit.
...
There's an exit.

WHY did you not say this **SOONER?**
I didn't want to be arrested the second I led you out! You're crazy ninja fast! I'm not taking my chances with that!

You could have just **LEFT ME HERE**.
GASP! We are almost sort of rival/friends! We're bonding and everything. And besides which, I have more class than that!

Class? Half your get-up is leather.
Your entire get-up is spandex.
You seem to like it.
I actually do a lot.

Can we have fun? Sexy fun? Before we go? Because we have time and you really are quite hot and I don't know when we'll be meeting up again where you're not trying to kick my ass.
This is true.

Make a good case and I'll think about it.

Okay.
Okay.
Good job.
Case won.

Do I get a reward?
Depends.
On?
How you feel about my packer.

We could just go back to kissing if you want. That was good.

OR, I can give you a very nice blowjob. I give great blowjobs. Five stars. Very showy. But if that's not going to do anything for you—

Yes. Please. That would be good.

Cold cold cold!
Ice for hands. Bad?
Surprising. Keep going.

You have such a nice cock.
Well-behaved and everything.

Ha. That counts for a lot.
I had a buddy who was shopping around for a packer once. Some of our... mutual acquaintances... thought they could offer some great, unprecedented, features.

I don't even want to know.

Are you sure? They're very competitive. Not even a little curious what they'd have to offer?
AH! Ah hah.
No. Not even a little bit.
I don't need my dick tricked out.

Okay. Okay. Not one of our guys. But one of yours maybe—?
Hah.
I WORK with those people. HOW EXACTLY is that conversation supposed to go?
Besides, our guys are just as crazy as yours. They'd probably try to give it lasers or something.
HA!

Anyways. You seem to be doing just fine with what I've got.

Ahh. You're almost complimentary when you're horny.
And it IS a nice cock.

Can your feel anything on your scars?
Not a lot.

I like it when people pay attention to them, though.
I tend to be proud of all my scars.

You... dig scars?

They're pretty fantastic.
Oh man. If you like scars—!
You have a few to share?
More than a few. But THIS GUY—

You ever hear of Incendio? Dude nearly blew my ass apart.
I remember the news coverage.
It was AMAZING! I mean, it sucked a whole lot—

Um—
I've ruined this, haven't I?

Okay?
Yea-
YEAH!
Very
okay!
Does it
hurt?
Just sore
and itchy
sometimes.
But it happened
ages ago. A lackey
lifestyle keeps me
active, mobile, and
stretching. Plus,
having ice for
hands comes with
its perks.
But you'd
tell me if it
hurt.
Sure
would.

Yeah?

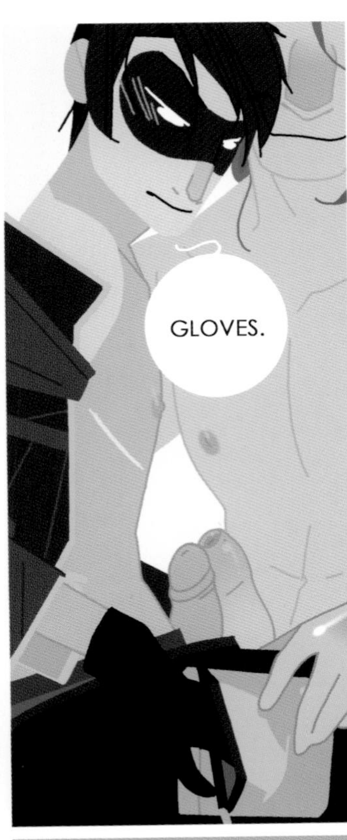
GLOVES.

Right. Right.
Ice and sensitive insides. I am not a monster.

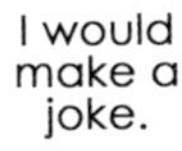
I would make a joke.

How generous!

Wait—

Do you have lube somewhere on your person too? You would, wouldn't you? Who carries condoms in their utility pockets?
Should I be having lube—?

You were real sexy half a second ago.

Don't sabotage yourself.

Hey! I am a gentle and sensitive lover!

Well, rough is a little nice too. Get to it.

Jee-sus. You're so warm.

Ah-ah-ha. That's mean. A throat like that is cheating.

Do it again.

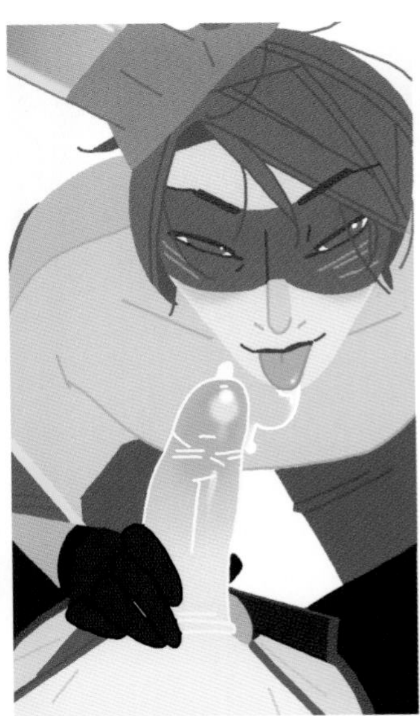

Uh-huh!

FUCKKK!

Hey. Hey.
Look up before you come. I know you're close. Show me? Please?

Hahhh-!

Ahhh.

That was nice.

Should do it again some time.
YEAH?!

CLANG!
!!!

WONDER?!
Go! Go! Go!
Call me. Call me. Call me.

I'm here!
SLAM!
?!?!

kisses.

Malcolm Easley
Alias: Wonder

Abilities:
Well-trained acrobat. Highly intelligent. Proficient in multiple fighting disciplines.

Temperament:
Wonder is reliable in any category of emergency. He utilizes stealth and strategy with such talent that he is a capable combatant against any foe.

He has a superpower. His superpower is not putting up with your shit.

Jack F.
Alias: Freezer Burn

Abilities:
Jack's hands are frozen solid ice until about his middle forearm. However, with exertion, the ice will move up as far as his shoulders. These hands can be used to chill or freeze on contact with Jack's discretion.

Jack is also physically strong, but not outside the norms of human strength.

Temperament:
Jack will loan his services out to the highest bidder, within reason. However, in the event of the truly catastrophic, Jack can be depended upon to render aid and assistance to the lawful.

CHAPTER 2

THE PRE-FUCK

Uh.
Alexei.
Sit down.

Did someone die?
No.
Is the world in imminent, unresolvable danger of ending?
No.
Sit down.
Amelia... are we breaking u—?
OH GOOD LORD, **NO.**
We are good. THINGS are satisfactory...
OH THANK GOD—
...so I thought it was time to negotiate the pre-fuck.

You'd think I'd be able to get a read on you by now—
*
The what?
The Pre-Fuck Negotiations.
The name is crude, but appropriate. It's like a Pre-Nup for sex.
Things are going well between us. It's reasonable to assume sex of some form will happen.
I want to encourage this progress. But only so long as we both have a clear understanding of the other person's positions on the matter.
Oh.
Okay.
I'm... for it?
Excellent. Let's proceed.
Let's start with the practicalities then. Sexual history, proclivities, and hard stops.
Ah.

Sorry. I was worried a bit. You're not usually SO procedural outside of work.
You said you liked my thoroughness.
I DO. It was especially cute when you asked me out.
I had been nervous.

...
Are you nervous now? You don't need to be....

It's not like it's anyone's first time.

NO. *Really?*

Whichbrings ustothesexual historyportion ofthisdiscussion.
Never?
I have no previous partners. And y—
How strict is the definition of "sex" we are using here—?
NO PARTNERS. And y—
So I'll be—
MY. FIRST. AND. YOU?

Hooow—?
IT JUST DID NOT **HAPPEN.**

I just didn't have the time!
First it was getting through high school with as many scholarships as possible. Then it was getting through college with as many credits as possible. Then it was my career and promotions and team building.
Becoming a superhero coordinator and tactician requires SERIOUS FOCUS. There wasn't any time for PEOPLE. Or THINGS.
AND SO IT DID. NOT. HAPPEN.

I know it's statistically abnormal, but—
It makes sense.

Hm.
WHAT?

Statistically abnormal, huh?
What, did you have this all planned out on timetables?

...
You do. Don't you?
It's a very flexible timetable.

Hey. I like you, okay? It's fine.
Let's discuss.

Thank you.
Ahem. How extensive is your sexual history? I don't need specifics if it makes you uncomfortable....
Nope! More than a few casual hookups. Three serious partners. Two women and one man.
...sort of? Maybe? Male-identifying alien? Their gender markers are different...
Let's see... if they fertilized the ovum....
So it's reasonable to assume your genitalia is compatible with mine?
Yes.

And... your health?
...can you even get diseases? For the life of me, I have never seen you sick.
Not yet. But I don't want to jinx it.
I have tested between partners.
I am also negative.

You have access to all my medical files anyways, don't you? You could have helped yourself.
Want anything from the fridge?
Those are for emergencies only! It would be a violation of your trust! And no. Thank you.

And... your superior strength. It posed no... problems...?

I didn't crush any bones. And I only left marks when they wanted me to.

...
Let's move on to the hard stops.

I have no idea what that means.
Things we know that we would not enjoy.

Oh. Well... let me think—
snk!
These are mine.
These are things people actually do?
I have seen all corners of the Internet. I assure you, each of these activities have their own devoted community.
This one has to be made up.
It's not.
There's no way—
I can get pictures.
Please don't.
Yes. Well. I don't have a written list. But this is a good place to start.
You WILL tell me if there's something you don't like that isn't on the list.
Yes. Yes, I will.

It's not on the list, but—

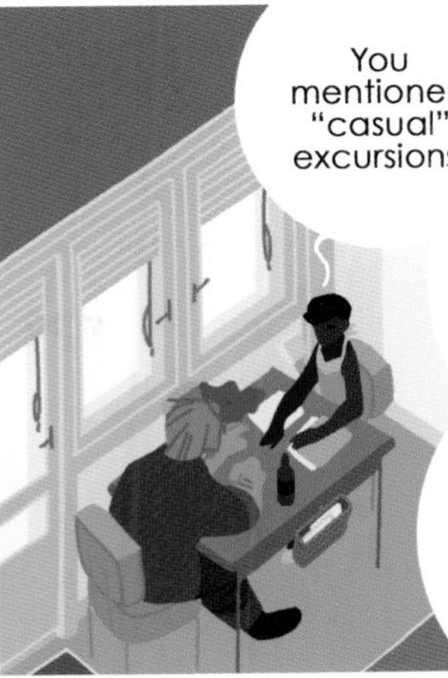
You mentioned "casual" excursions.
Inhale. I have no interest in anything outside of monogamy.
It is best that, should you want something outside those parameters, we should address the subject now before—

Hon.
You're adorable. You're capable. You sometimes terrify me.
You are a lovely partner. I'll seek no others while you'll have me.

Sometimes that isn't why it happens, though.
I want you to be honest if that's something you want. I'll only be mad if you don't tell me....

If I start thinking differently about our relationship, I'll tell you.

I just—
I waited such a long time. I don't want to screw this up—
You're doing fine.

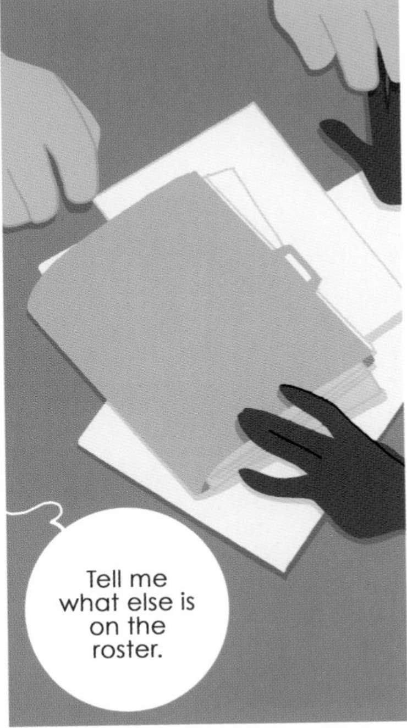
Tell me what else is on the roster.

...
Since I have no practical experience, and what people fantasize about doesn't always line up with what they like realistically, I have no CERTAIN interests.
But...
...I have assembled a list of things I would be willing to try.
And of course, I welcome any discussion as to what you might like.
A comprehensive kink list. So helpful!
This is... VERY comprehensive.
I'm a virgin. Not an innocent.

Kitten
play?
It's... *ahem.*
When one or both
partners act as
though they
are cats.
Well.
The broader term
is pet play. There
are puppies and
ponies too. It can
get quite involved,
actually.
You can
buy collars. Ears.
Tails on garters. Tails on
butt plugs. Muzzles and
bridles. There are gloves
that act like hooves
or paws.
The cat ones
come with claws
on them, even.
Although... it could
be just as simple as
someone getting a
belly rub—
Ahem. Who is
the cat? ...in this
scenario?

...
Me.
Cough.
I see.

So, my role would be... owner? Caretaker?
...both, I suppose?
There's a... niceness... to being taken care of. To have someone else lead.
Mph.
That is a very nice idea.
!
Should we discuss it more in depth?
Would you tell me you're dressing up or down in advance?
Or would I just come home to you curled up on the couch? With nothing on but a COLLAR and TAIL.

SHOULD we imagine that NOW?
I need a verbal answer.
yes
Ahem. Yes, please.
WOULD you wear a tail? I'd love to see one on you.
A garter's fine, but one with a plug would look sooo much better. And imagine how it'd FEEL.
Plugs were on the MAYBE list, right? Could we? I'd make it worth it. I'd find a beautiful fluffy one. Like a Persian. Do they make those? It'd feel so soft.
Can... can I have a black one? Please?
Of course. Anything you want. I'll take care of everything. And I'd be dying to take care of you. To put my hands on you. I'd start at your scalp.
There's this spot, just at the back of the head. Feels so good to get a nice strong tug, right there. You'd love it. I promise.

At some point I'd have to have you lay across my lap. Belly up. Like you're sunning yourself.
whimper

My thumbs would stroke nice deep circles, starting at your neck.
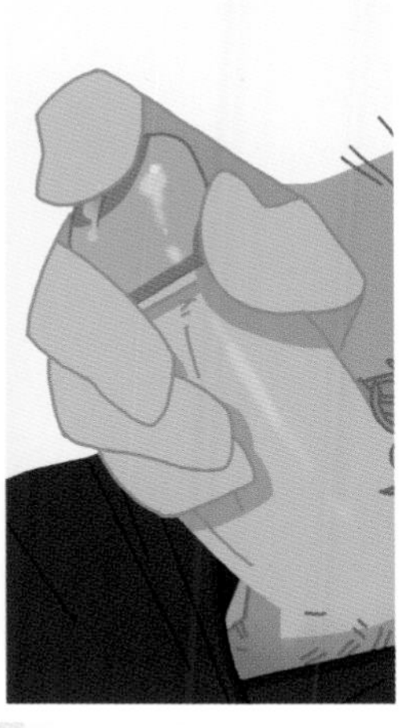

I could bring my hands down around your ribs. I'd pet the lines of them as they bring me down to your stomach.

I think you'd twitch the lower I got.
Do you think I could make you purr?

I bet you'd be restless.
OF COURSE you'd be restless.
Look at you now. I haven't even touched you and you're already overwhelmed. And it looks SO GOOD on you.

When I finally get my hands lower, you'll be all worked up.
I'd have to tease you, though. Just a little.
Because GOD. You look so good like this, and I'd keep you worked up forever if you wouldn't tear my head off for it.
I'd pull at your tail through the "V" of my fingers.
And then I'd pull.
Not enough to pull out your tail, but just enough to make you FEEL it.
And I'd make up for all this teasing, of course. I don't want my KITTEN—
ah.
—to be angry with me.
I'd put my hand back to the base of your tail. Push my thumb in at the rim, where the skin juuust holds, and then stroke the edge of it.

You'd be so sensitive by then. And full.
Does that sound nice?
yes
Such a lovely kitten.
Do you think that'll be enough? Or would you want more? I think you'd DESERVE more.
please?
It's not enough attention.
Not when I could have my fingers IN you.
I'd have one hand back at the base of your skull. Massaging nice and hard.
And with the other hand—
Ah!
These fingers? Don't they feel nice? Strong and warm? Think about how good they'd be between your legs.
You'd be wet.
Are you wet now? You look like you might be.
God, you'd be so soft and warm.

Goddd. I want to see you like that. I want to HAVE you like that.

I'm so hard thinking about it NOW.

I'd push my fingers in fast, just to jolt you a little. See if I can't make you yowl.

You'd be close. Your eyes would be closed and your mouth in a perfect "O."

I'd find all the best ways to make you purr.

Every noise you'd make would go straight to my cock.

How do you think you'd like it, Kitten? Hard and deep?

I'd find the deepest parts of you. And PRESS.

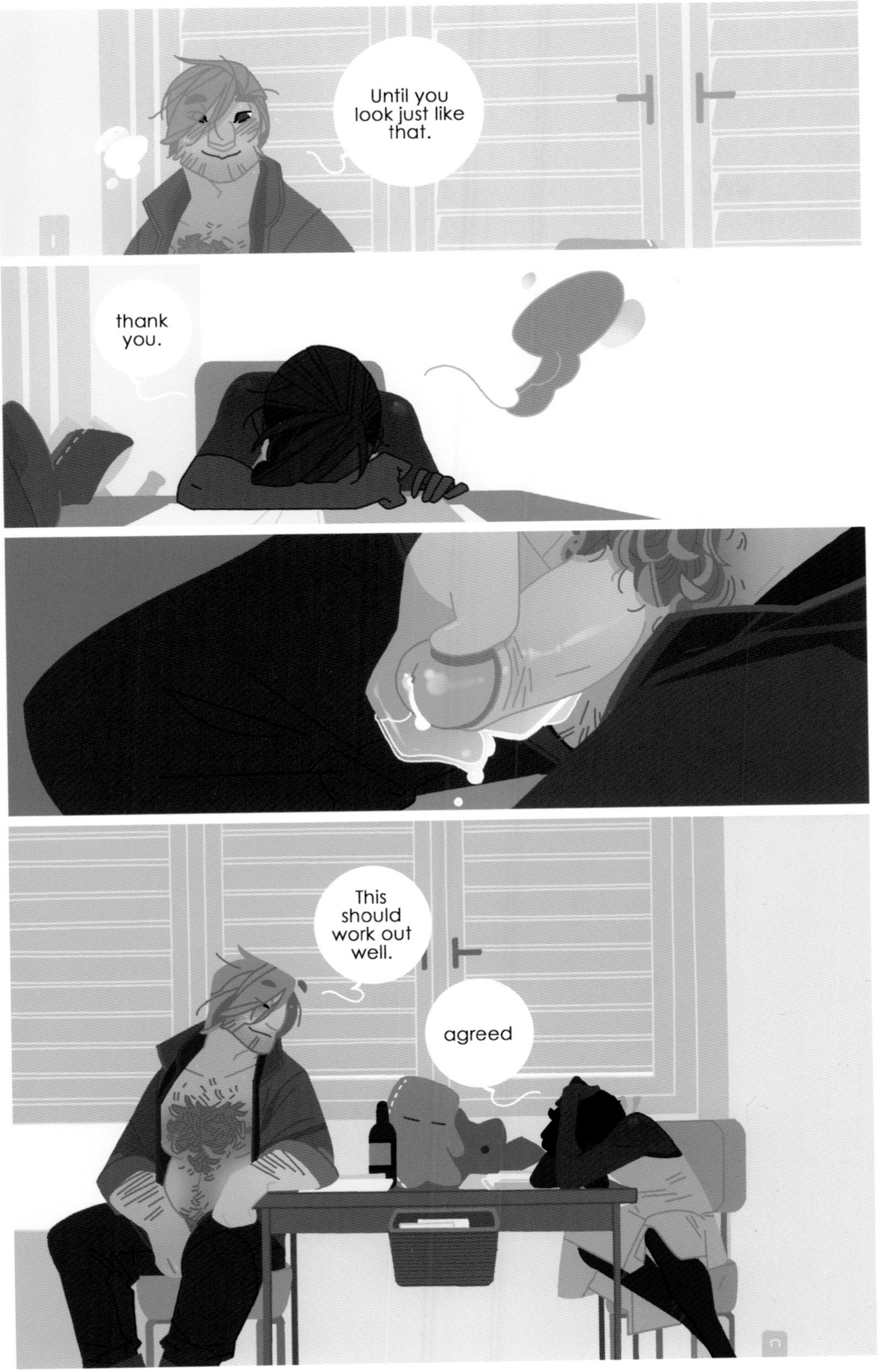

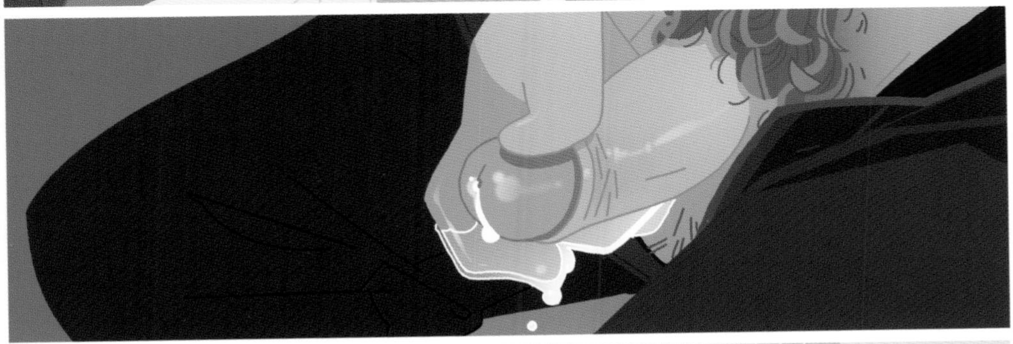

This should work out well.

agreed

Amelia Brown

Abilities:
Expert tactician and
intel collector

Ms. Brown is efficient,
dependable, and cowed
by no one, be they human,
alien, mythical, or celestial.
She is fluent in two interstellar
languages and regularly relied
upon to negotiate treaties and
prisoner exchanges on behalf
of Earth.

Please do not provoke her.

Alexei Golokov
Alias: Titan

Abilities:
Strongman class superhero
Extreme durability

Alexei is an interstellar
citizen, splitting time between
Earth and his home world.
Initially he was raised on Earth
due to the political climate on
his home world, but he returned
in his adolescence to pursue
training to become an
intergalactic peacekeeper.

When you're as strong as Titan,
you really don't have to pay
much attention to what people
think of you. Which is how
Alexei comes to be so open
about a ridiculously strong
obsession with adorable toys.

Nations have tried to curry
Titan's favor with these toys.
Japan even commissioned a
limited edition "Hello Cat" Titan
costume. He loves it.

Amelia!
Amelia!
Laser cats!
They have
honest to god
laser cats!

CHAPTER 3

GOOD FOUNDATIONS

ALIAS #3
SNITCH
MOM

Okay, Owen, honey. Talk.

I'm here. You're here. You don't have to worry about anyone else being here.

You need to start talking about what's freaking you out. I've seen it affecting your work. I've seen it affecting YOU. And… you don't HAVE to tell me, necessarily, whatever it is. But you don't have to be AFRAID of telling me either.

Unless you're afraid of ME?!

It's nothing you did or do.
It's something I do.
And I'm worried you'll hate it.
Sweetheart. We're super-villains. That could mean anything.
But—
Of the two of us, most people would have their money on me, the mad scientist, as the more likely cause of whatever would make this relationship go south.
And that is being EXTREMELY generous. To me. By me.

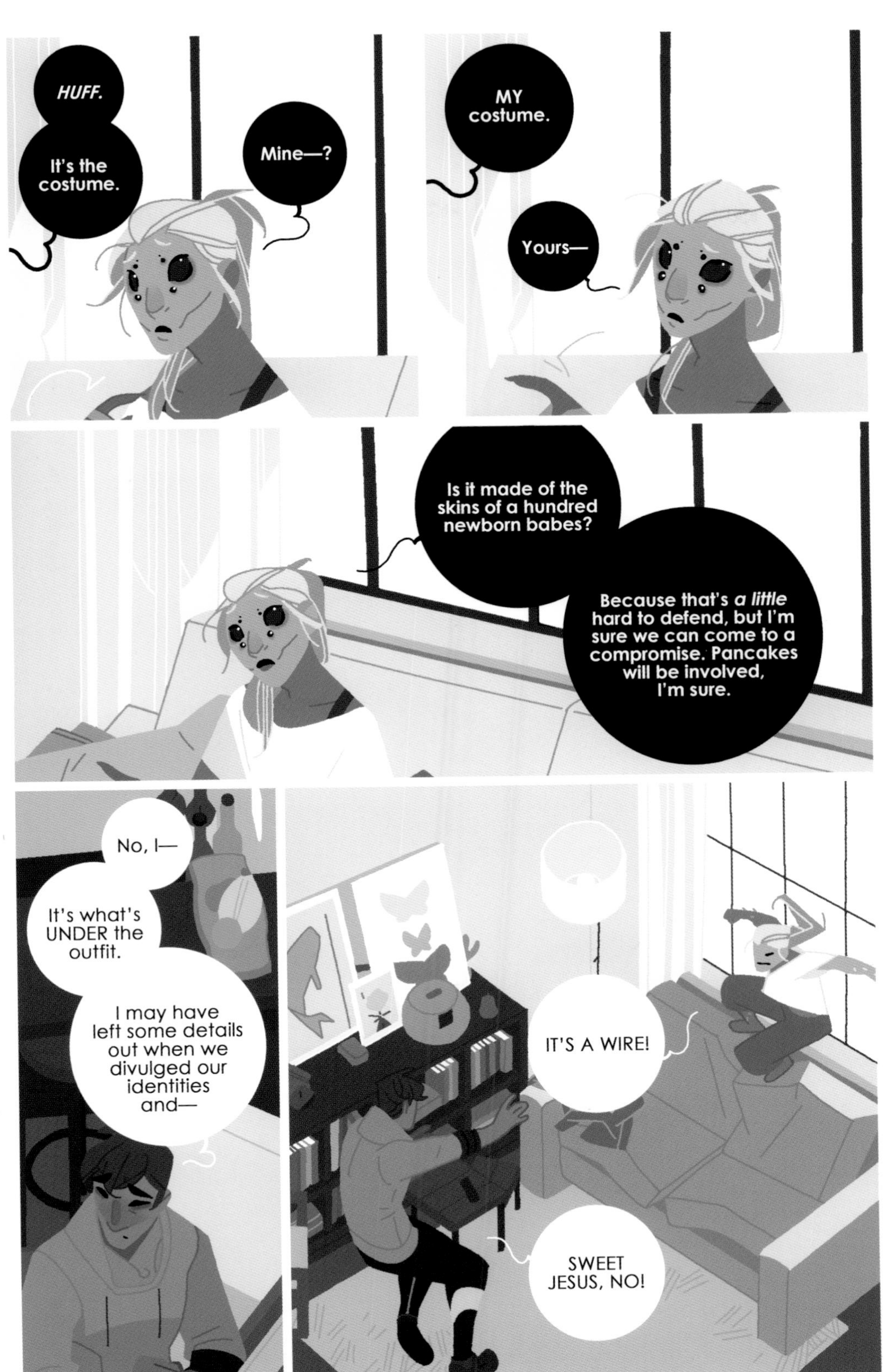
HUFF.
It's the costume.
Mine—?
MY costume.
Yours—
Is it made of the skins of a hundred newborn babes?
Because that's *a little* hard to defend, but I'm sure we can come to a compromise. Pancakes will be involved, I'm sure.
No, I—
It's what's UNDER the outfit.
I may have left some details out when we divulged our identities and—
IT'S A WIRE!
SWEET JESUS, NO!

That outfit doesn't leave much room FOR anything else.
What else COULD you be hiding under there? A SECOND secret identity?
Owen Moreau: Twice secretive, much alias?
Look. Okay. Yes. I'll just—

Oh.
Um. Ha.
Wow.
I always thought you had a more pronounced hip to chest ration with the costume on. I just figured the black was slimming.
That's not really funny right now....
NO!
Nope, you are right, it absolutely is not funny. I am sorry.
Oh honey, c'mere.

I'm sorry
I made you
anxious.

I probably could have done this better, but you were the first person I've ever told and I worried....
Aw, honey, come sit.

I'm so happy you trusted me enough to tell me, sweet thing.

If you hadn't told me, I wouldn't have known how pretty you are like this.
Although I should have probably guessed. A thief WOULD have an eye for beautiful things.
How often do you wear these?
...under my costume. When I can. If the job's not too difficult.
Because it feels nice? Because it feels pretty? Or because it feels a little sexy?
Nice. Mostly. Sexy too though... sometimes.
Oh?
Could it be a bit sexy now?
It might be getting there.

I think we can make it nice AND sexy, baby boy.
mph.
No?
Baby boy...
or baby... girl?
This wasn't something I meant to talk about today!

Nothing to be ashamed of, sweetpea.
I didn't think the conversation would go this way....
We don't have to have the conversation now if you don't want to.
We can still have a good time. And you can still be my girl while we're having it, if that's something you'd like.
I just don't want to make things weird right this second. We were having a good time.
My very pretty girl.
Who's slim and full in all these pretty places.
And all wrapped up in bows.
Is that something you'd like?
Yeah. Yeah, it is.
You're sure this doesn't...
...bother you?

I could keep going.
But only if YOU still want to.
Ah! I really, really do.
Good. Because I want to make you feel so, so good.
Because I love that you look so, so gorgeous. And I REALLY think that should be encouraged.
Maybe I can even help you shop sometime? Buy you a present?
A nice little teddy, I think.

Good?

A lot better than I thought this would go....
But good?

So good.

I could get used to this.

We could go out. Have fun. And all the while I'll know that I've got such a sweet baby girl beside me, all dressed up underneath her clothes.

And you would be, right? My sweet baby girl?
I LIKE my girl when she's SWEET.
I would be, for you.
Good girl.
Ah! Please!

...please.

Oh god!

Good?
Yes. More. Please.

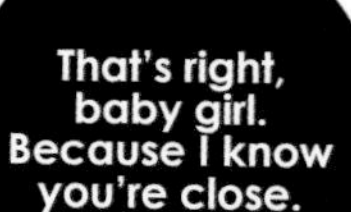

That's right, baby girl. Because I know you're close.
I want to see my baby girl come when she's dressed up so prettily.

And you. You too.
Such a sweetheart. Thinking of me.

Hnnnn!
Mph!

So...
...you're really okay with this?
Is being my baby girl something you want from me?
Yes. Maybe. Sometimes.
Just in the bedroom?
...no
Outside. Too. Sometimes.
Sometimes I feel like a boy. Sometimes I feel like a girl. Sometimes I don't feel like either....
Does that... does *this* bother you?

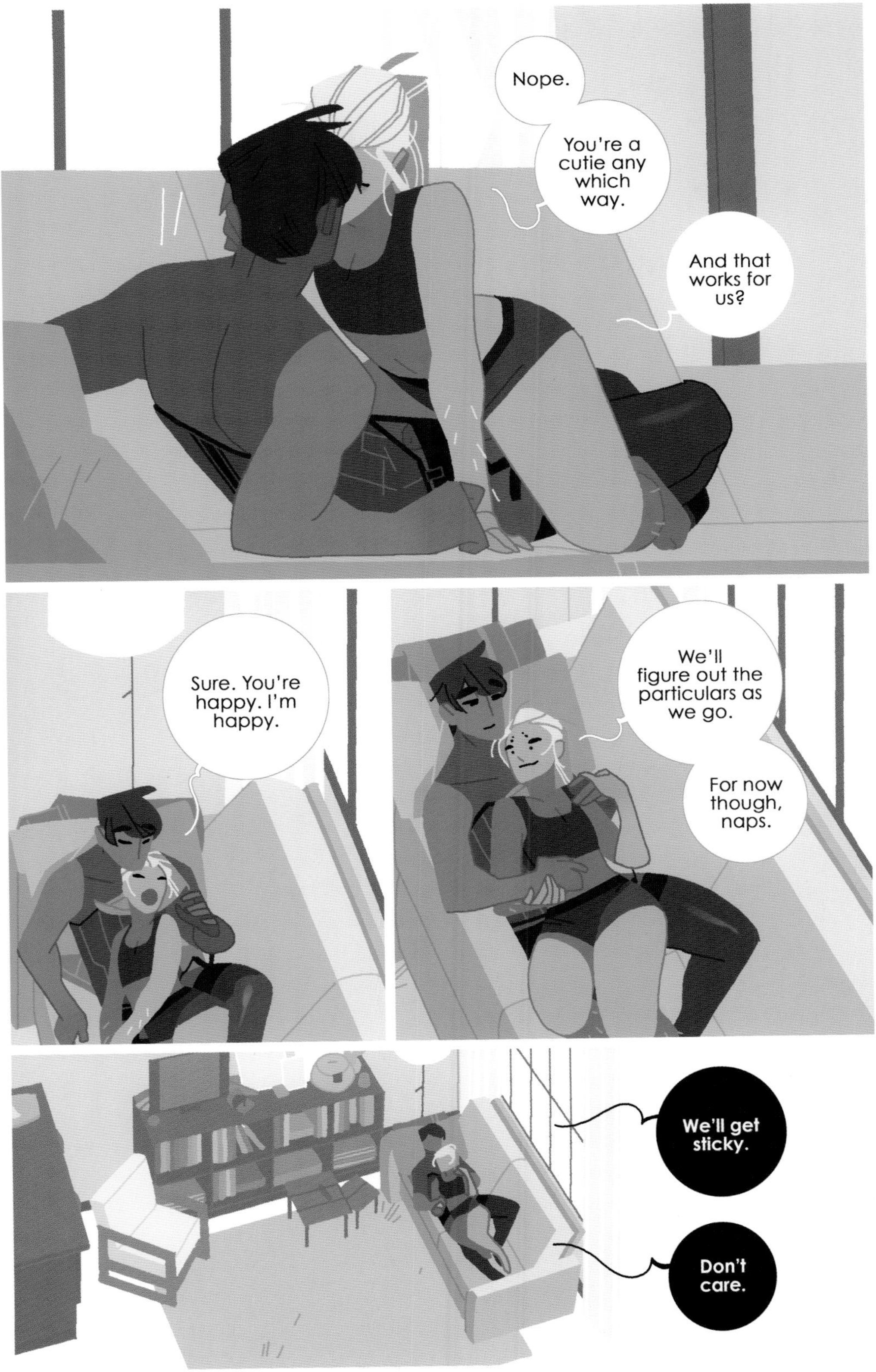

Nope.

You're a cutie any which way.

And that works for us?

Sure. You're happy. I'm happy.

We'll figure out the particulars as we go.

For now though, naps.

Owen Moreau
Alias: Shade
Abilities:
Agility and strong acrobatics training.
Owen Moreau is an adept thief with an eye for art.
Owen Moreau is more or less every museum's worst nightmare. He'll steal for profit, pleasure, and (to the delight and despair of many) to repatriate pieces back to their country of origin. Which ALWAYS results in international clusterfucks.
(So far, no museum has successfully argued for the right to get any of those said pieces back.)
When not terrorizing art museums, he's working for them in art restoration.
Charlotte Colt
Alias: Recluse
Abilities:
Spider-like adaptations such as sensitivity to vibrations, venom, multiple eyes, and setules (fine hairs on her hands and feet that allow for climbing on virtually any surface).
Charlotte will neither confirm nor deny whether she makes spider silk. And it would probably be a mistake to ask her.
Charlotte is an accomplished biochemist with a strong suit in non-lethal poisons. She'd be invaluable to the scientific community, if not for her own distinct rationale as to how such sciences should be applied....

CHAPTER 4

SAFE

So, I'll be coming through the window.... Do we want to address the window lock? I assume we are suspending disbelief and PRETENDING I broke it.
No property damage. Cheap stuff is fair game, but void my security deposit at your own risk.
But your lingerie—
Go wild.
I'm going to use my fingers to cut it. Or are we keeping powers out of this?
Powers are fine. I trust you.
Tell me how you'll let me know if the breathplay is too much.
Snap my fingers.
And the safe word?
SPECULUM.
Yes. That'll kill a mood.

Cora, you WILL safeword if this gets to be too much. You don't have to prove anything by sticking with this if it sucks.
It'll be fine, Kavi. I've been daydreaming about this for AGES.
That doesn't mean you'll like it WHEN IT'S ACTUALLY HAPPENING. People fantasize about things all the time that they'd hate in reality.
You have to be prepared for the idea that it might not live up to expectations. It could be scary. This isn't exactly the most comforting scenario we're playing with here.
You've been researching, haven't you?
CORA. Promise me, right now, that you will safeword, if need be.
I promise.
This'll be hot, though. I will probably go cross-eyed from all the sexy.
Hrm.

THUMP thump!

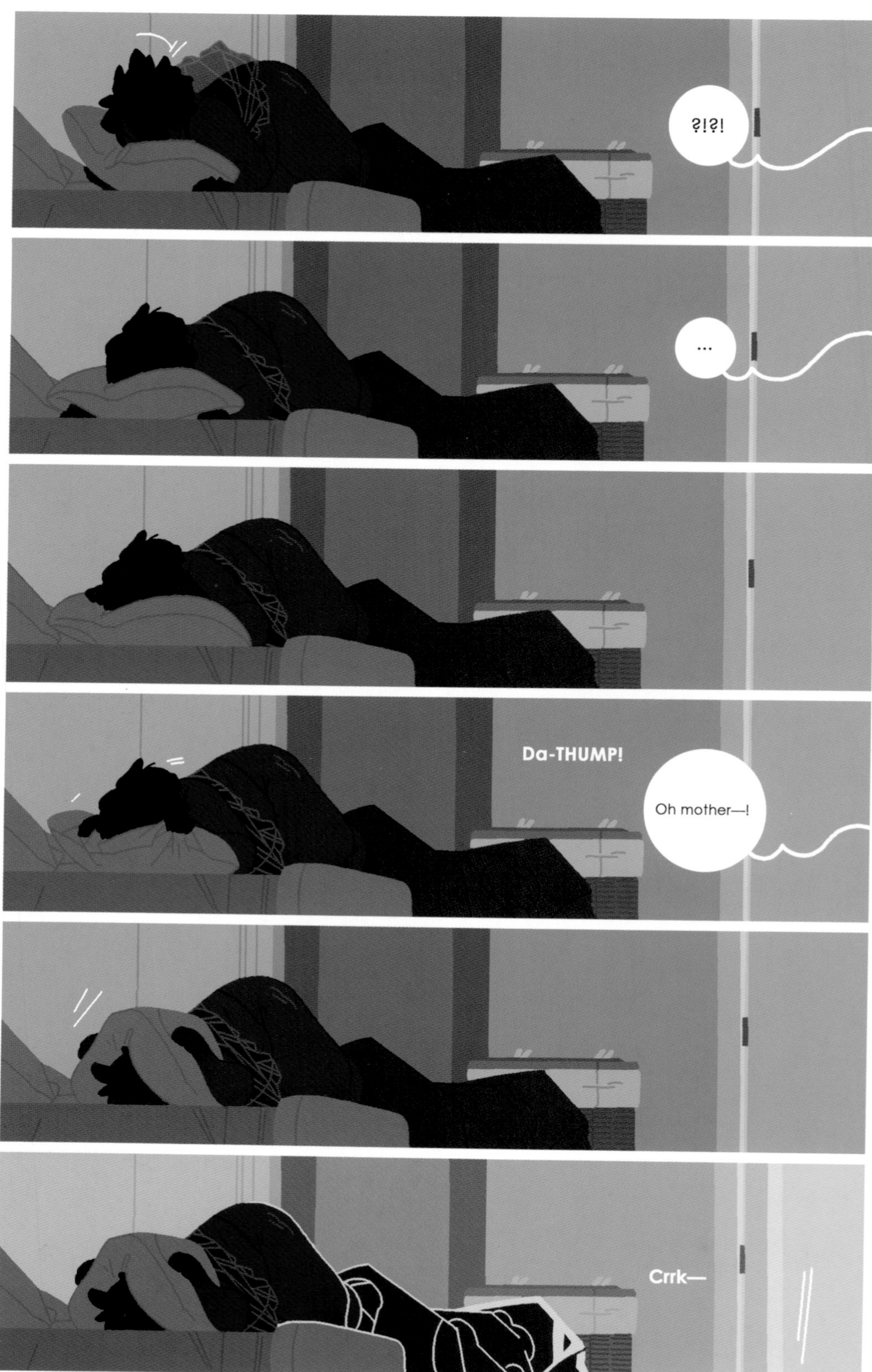
¿!¿!
...
Da-THUMP!
Oh mother—!
Crrk—

?!!

!!!

C—
-Ahem-
Hello, Cora Jenkins.
CLEAVE!

Indeed.
Don't do anything silly now.

You know what I can do.

Oh, this is nice.
So, Cora.
May I call you Cora? CONTACT seems so formal. And Ms. Jenkins is a bit impersonal, don't you think?
What do you want—? HOW did you even FIND me?

I've been watching. You caught my attention. And you're not nearly careful enough. Any ol' creeper could have found their way in here...
and seen you like this....

You look like you crave a CERTAIN SOMETHING like this. And I think I can give it to you.
YOU'RE JOKING.
I'm really not.
And frankly—

You're not really in the best position to argue.

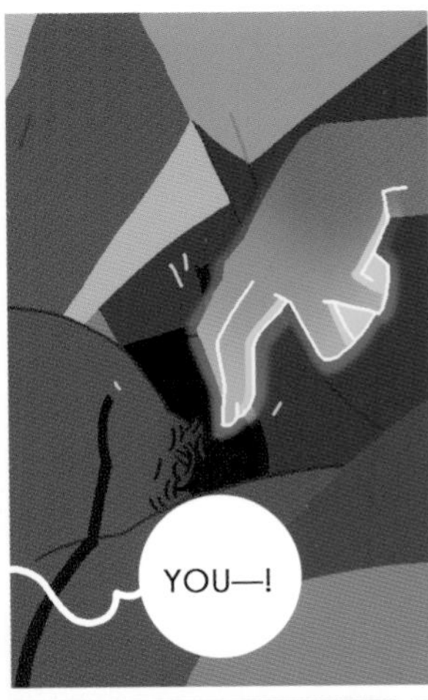
YOU—!

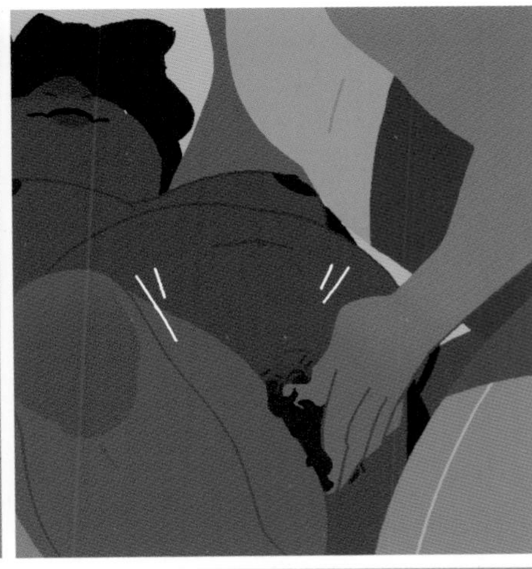

I could make it good. I WANT to make it good.

You'd like it.

NO! No. No. No. No. NOT HAPPENING. GET OFF!
FINE.

Wha— Really?

NOPE.

Now be good. Before I have to gag you, too.
Where were we?

Oh, yes.

FUN.
Ah—!

Shhh. Shh.
This doesn't have to be a trial. This can be GOOD.

I've spent A LOT of time thinking about it.

Ah—!

CAT!
Wha—?
Mao.

CAT.

?
Cat. Cat.
Cat. Cat.
Cat. Cat.

OUT.
Mao.

Inhale.

I don't LIKE being interrupted.

And I don't LIKE being denied.
Mm.
...

And... and shame on you for having a cat in the bedroom.

Was—was that supposed to be a slap?
I....

Slap!
AH!

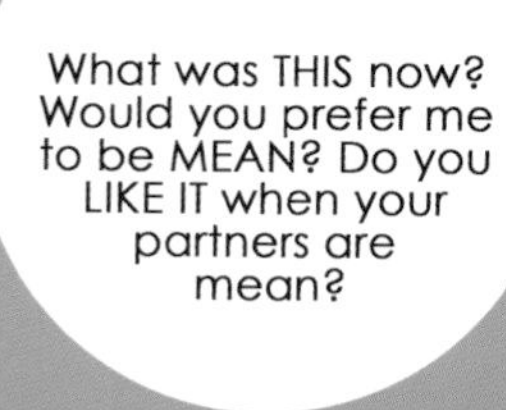
What was THIS now? Would you prefer me to be MEAN? Do you LIKE IT when your partners are mean?

Because I can be VERY mean.

Please!

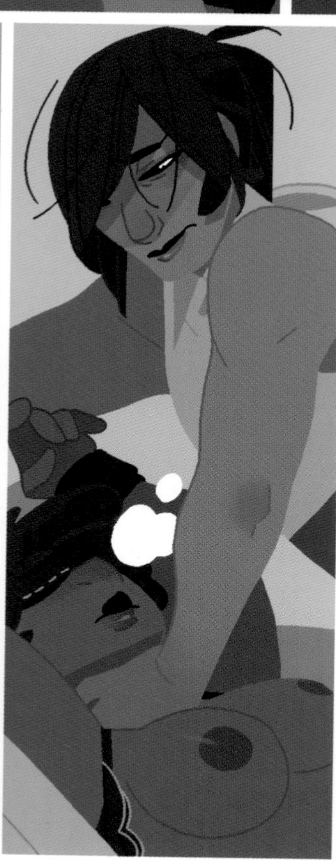

Speculum.

Fuck.
Kavi?

I don't like this and I'm not good at this...

...and it feels scary even though you're okay. But what if you're not? And what if you panicked and couldn't safeword? What if I read it wrong?
Shh. Shh.

We can stop....

...

We don't HAVE to keep going.
But you wanted to.
If we're up to it, we can try it again later. If we're not, we won't. It's clear there was a lot we weren't prepared for.
And besides, it's just a fantasy. Our sex life does not hinge on our ability to role play.

... I was REALLY bad at this though.
Snrk

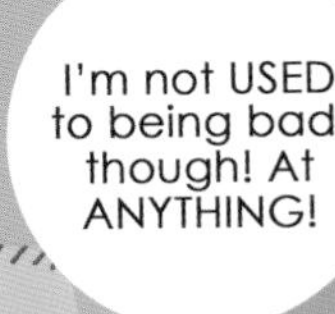

I'm not USED to being bad, though! At ANYTHING!
Hah!
You are NOT being supportive. This is a serious blow to my ego.

This CANNOT be allowed to happen again.
I MUST DO SCIENCE.
HAH HA HA!
HA! We needed a trial run to sex!
Your stealth was awful!
If you had CLEANED a bit better, I wouldn't have hit everything you put in my way.

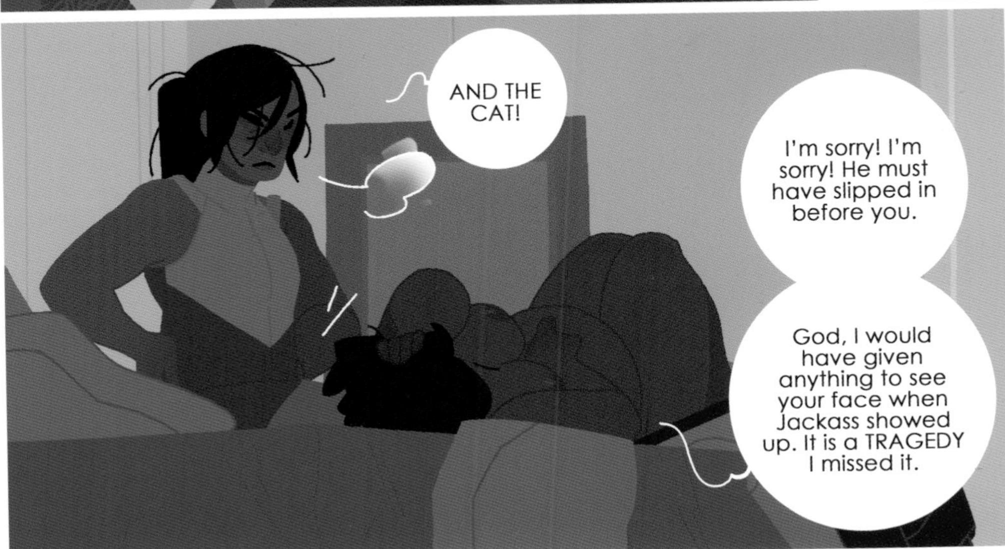
AND THE CAT!
I'm sorry! I'm sorry! He must have slipped in before you.
God, I would have given anything to see your face when Jackass showed up. It is a TRAGEDY I missed it.

It was not my most dignified moment.

...you really don't mind?
Nope!

But you were really excited.
Yes—

—and it's JUST A SHAME that I don't have a CAREFULLY CURATED, EXTENSIVE COLLECTION of trashy romance novels for all my bodice-ripping needs.

Hm.

Should we call it a night?

NO.
We wasted lingerie and a lamp tonight. We will not be denied.
That lingerie cost nothing and I got that lamp in a garage sale.

I am making a most generous offer to EAT YOU OUT and you're TURNING ME DOWN?

Get naked and get down there already.

Ah ha ha!

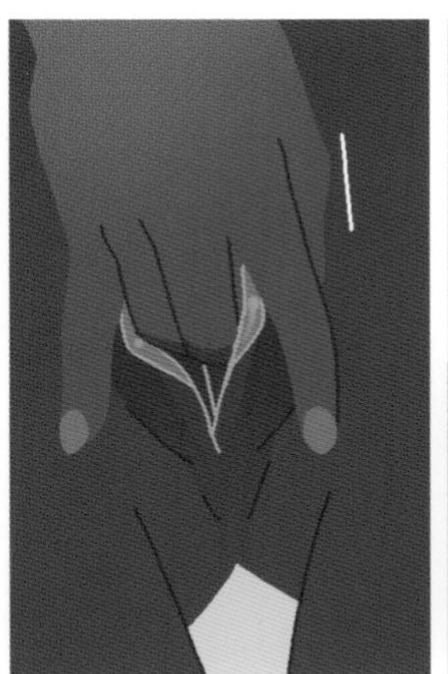

Ahhh
hhh—

!
OH
GOOOOOO
OOOD—!

Hah. Okay.
NOW we call
it a night.

You did good,
sweetheart.

Love
you.

Kavi Narang
Alias: Cleave
Abilities:
By making slashing gestures, Cleave's hands can cut through most materials. She can accomplish the same feat with kicks, but not to the same degree.
Cleave is nearly on the cusp of full-time heroing. Until then, she takes appointments as a personal fitness trainer.
A veteran perfectionist and unfailingly efficient, it's only a matter of time before she's tapped for a team.
She'll claw her way to a leadership from there.
Cora Jenkins
Alias: Contact
Abilities:
Contact can see an inanimate object's history through touch.
Officially a copy editor. Unofficially a moonlighting superheroine. Contact's ability to read an object's history (where it's been and who's had it) is exceptionally useful for intel gathering.
Although, personally, the ability has its drawbacks. She will never sleep in a hotel again.

CHAPTER 5

THE RESPONSIBLE PARTIES

ding!

Ding!

WHAT THE
HELL, MAN?!

$%*^@!

SLAM!

Grooooooaa
aannnnn....

You alive back there, kid?
...yesss?
Is that an answer or a question?

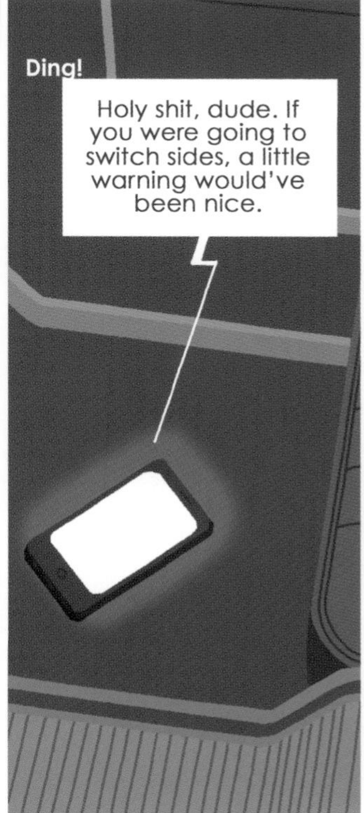
Ding!
Holy shit, dude. If you were going to switch sides, a little warning would've been nice.

...my muscles won't work right....
Yeah, tasers will do that.

...wha happened?
You ran your mouth off at some very bad people. Who were armed with some very good weapons. Including a taser net. Against which your super speed means jack shit.
And you are VERY LUCKY that someone hates them, coincidentally sending me after them at the same time.

What happened to them...?
Something very, very bad, I assure you.

Ding!
Wow, man, wow. Far be it from me to tell you how to live your life, but if you were going to take a protégé, you could've done waaayyy better than the speedster.

Holy shit, you're HUSH.
So nice to meet a fan.

Don't you kill people?
Depends on whether or not someone can prove it.

Ding!

Aren't you really old?
SIT DOWN AND PUT ON YOUR SEATBELT RIGHT NOW!

Ding!
I've been hearing some interesting rumors. Did you go soft on us, old man? >:)

Ding!
Ding!
Ding!

YOU KNOW WHERE I LIVE?!
I know where everyone lives. You aren't special.
Ding!

Ding!

Ding!

Ding!

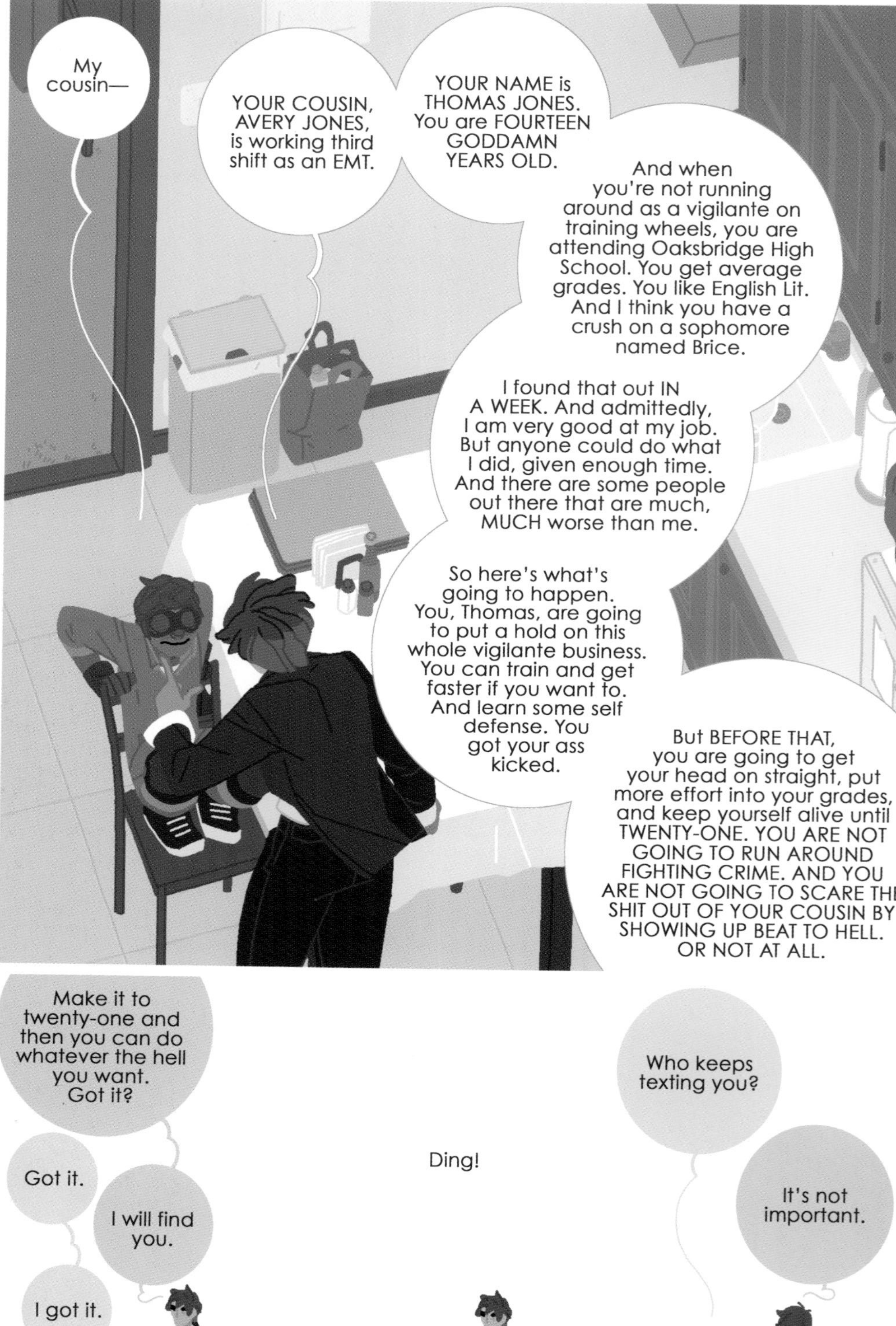
My cousin—
YOUR COUSIN, AVERY JONES, is working third shift as an EMT.
YOUR NAME is THOMAS JONES. You are FOURTEEN GODDAMN YEARS OLD.
And when you're not running around as a vigilante on training wheels, you are attending Oaksbridge High School. You get average grades. You like English Lit. And I think you have a crush on a sophomore named Brice.
I found that out IN A WEEK. And admittedly, I am very good at my job. But anyone could do what I did, given enough time. And there are some people out there that are much, MUCH worse than me.
So here's what's going to happen. You, Thomas, are going to put a hold on this whole vigilante business. You can train and get faster if you want to. And learn some self defense. You got your ass kicked.
But BEFORE THAT, you are going to get your head on straight, put more effort into your grades, and keep yourself alive until TWENTY-ONE. YOU ARE NOT GOING TO RUN AROUND FIGHTING CRIME. AND YOU ARE NOT GOING TO SCARE THE SHIT OUT OF YOUR COUSIN BY SHOWING UP BEAT TO HELL. OR NOT AT ALL.
Make it to twenty-one and then you can do whatever the hell you want. Got it?
Got it.
I will find you.
I got it.
Ding!
Who keeps texting you?
It's not important.

RIN—

I HAVE NOT GONE SOFT!

Okay.
How does that affect our dinner plans?

...
hello, dear.

I went to close tonight's "account." Everything was set up perfectly.

EXCEPT, supertween Speedster is already there. He TRIED to hit the crew, but only succeeded in getting his ass handed to him and stressing everyone out.

And the kid's okay! ...relatively. The taser hit is gonna smart for a while... but he's not being boiled in lye right now, so he can suck it up.

Honey, you know I hardly ever encourage this, but you CAN kill some of them.

WHAT DOES THAT MATTER IF NO ONE BELIEVES I CAN?!

I'm turning sixty.
Non-sequitur, but okay.

I'm turning sixty and everyone is expecting me to go soft. They were all waiting for it.
I am an old man. And everyone is waiting for me to retire.

Do you WANT to retire?

No. But that doesn't matter, does it?

You get married. You have a family. You get old. You get soft. It's all a trajectory towards befuddled old man who needs to be put to pasture.

You are not a dog, Elio. You are a hitman, with documented kills. Anyone stupid enough to think you're about to become an easy target would be dead before they hit the ground.

but—
No. Stop. Enough.
Come home so I can feed you and take care of you.

but—
NO. STOP. You're overstressed. You're overthinking. And you need to come home so I can help you clear your mind.

...howww?
I'm going to wreck you, sweetheart.

Hang up. Start the car. And come home.

This whole thing is going to ruin my credibility. Forever.
Shh. Your credibility is iron clad. You'll be fine.
But let's try and forget about that for a while.

!
ELIO.

You are going to look at me. You are going to pay attention to me. And you're going to let go of everything else.
Understood?

yes.
Ahem.
Dear.
Good boy.

I want to take care of you, because I think you've earned it.

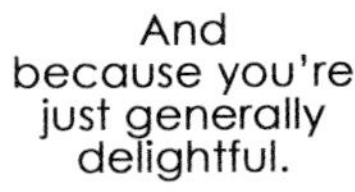
And because you're just generally delightful.

You did real good, looking out for that kid even though he doesn't know what's what yet.

There were, what? Five? Ten targets on this account?
Twelve. Dear.

TWELVE? You must have done VERY WELL. There isn't a mark on you.
Getting old. *PFT.*

Feels like
I fucked
up.
Huff.

Okay
then.

Hands on
the chair.

You can do
that for me,
right? Keep
your hands to
yourself for a
little while?

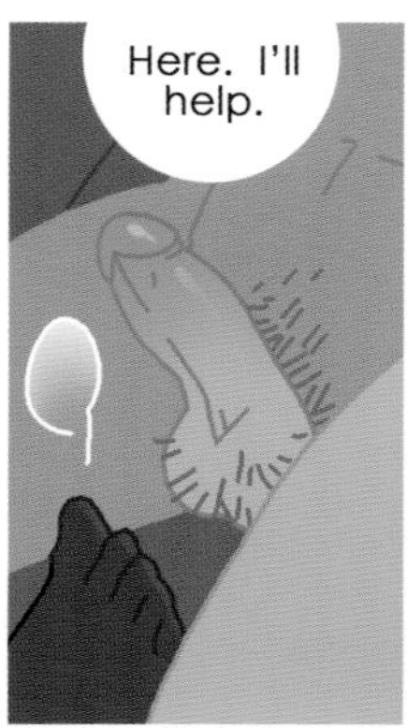
Here. I'll help.

No. Touching.

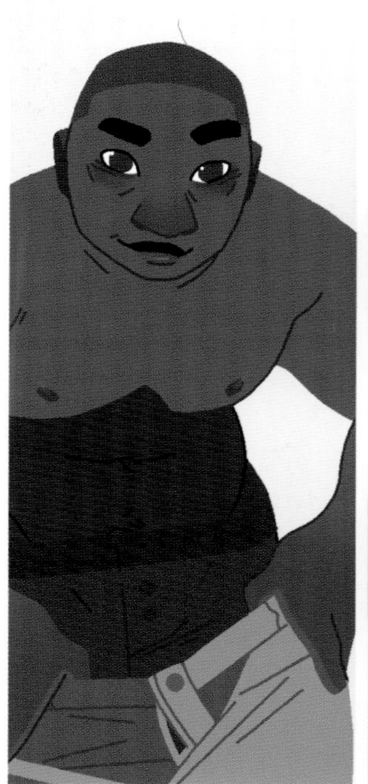
Hands on your seat.

We can use restraints if we need to.
But we don't have to, do we? You've already done so well tonight. You can behave a little while more, can't you?
Yes, dear.
That's my baby.

Now, I'm going to open myself up. And you're going to watch.

We're both going to enjoy this.

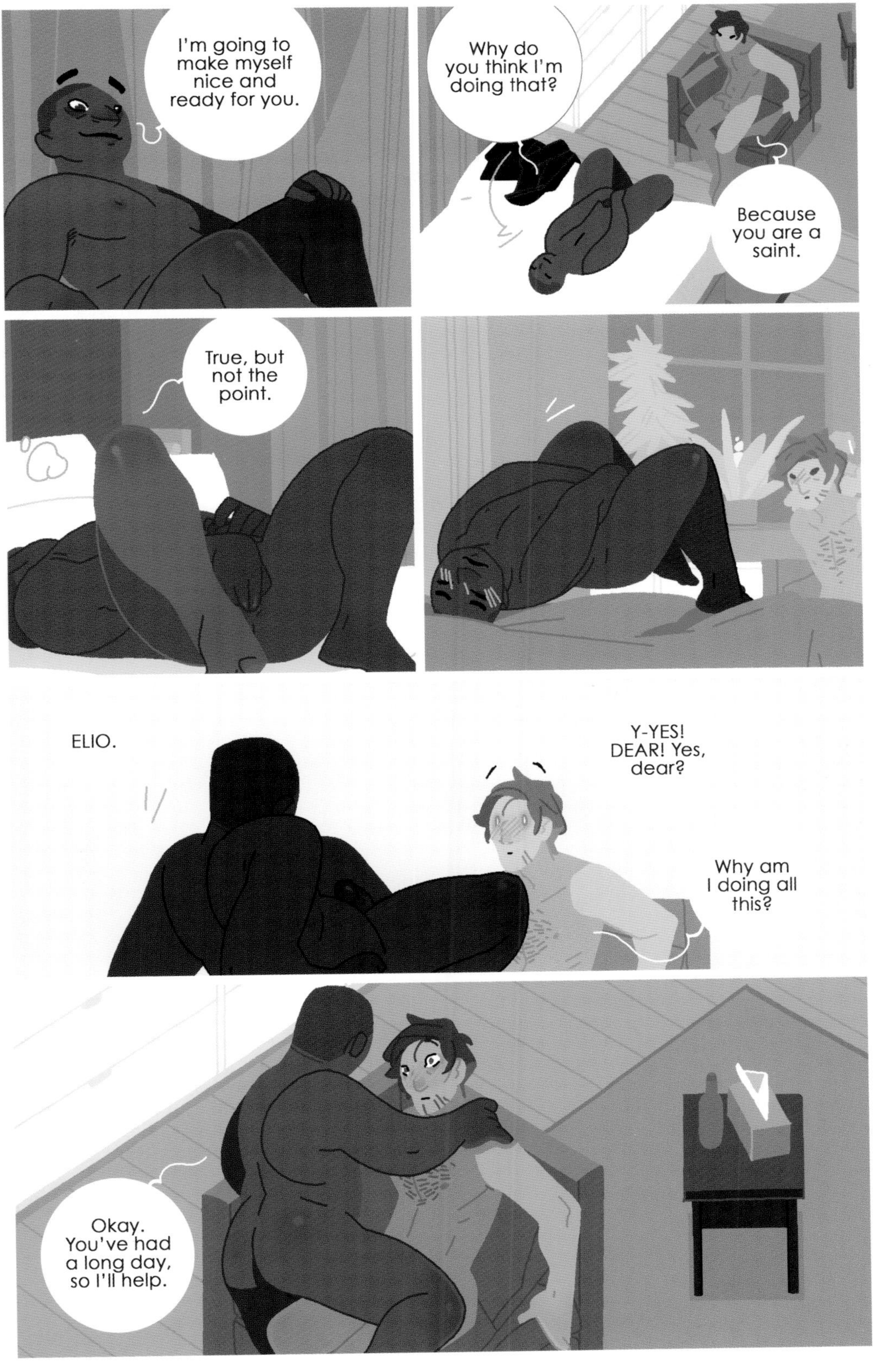

ELIO.

Y-YES! DEAR! Yes, dear?

Why am I doing all this?

Okay. You've had a long day, so I'll help.

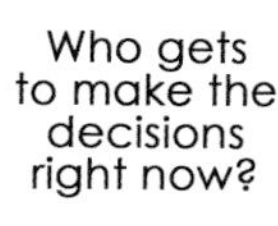

You do, dear.

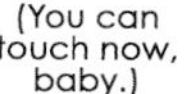

Do you get to argue with me right now?

No. *Hah.* Dear.

Then I think that means you've done well. Do you agree with me, that you've done well? Because if you want this, if you want to keep feeling good, you have to agree with me.
Yes. I want— I do—
Then I think you should come.

Nnnh!

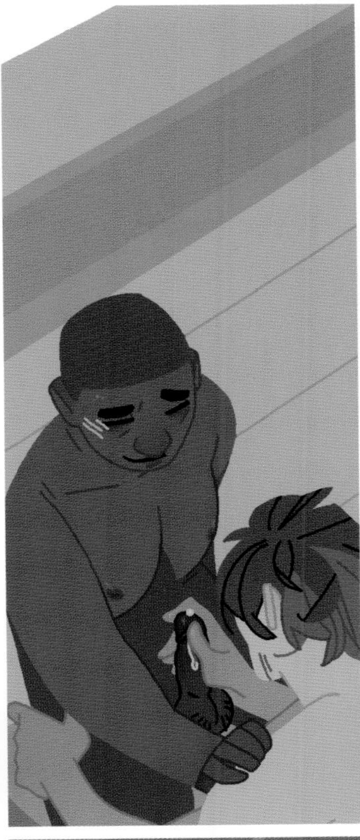

Ah—!

Hah... Good job, dear.
Mmm.

Let's get you cleaned up and put to bed.
mm. thank you. love you. best husband.

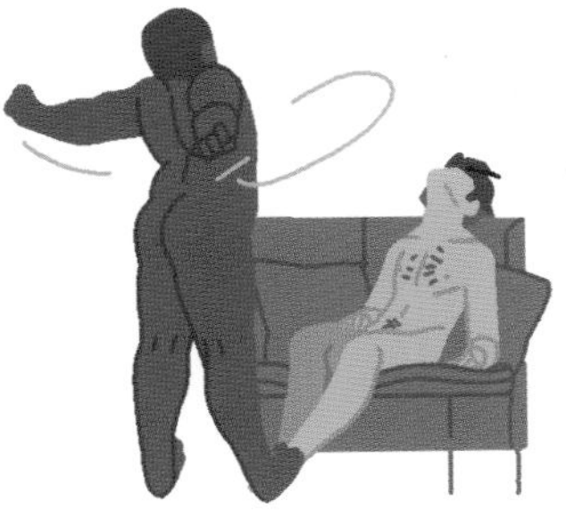

Samuel De León
Classified:
Civilian
Samuel De León has the exceptional distinction of intimidating a grown-ass assassin. Mostly by utilizing the "you have disappointed me more than any living creature in the whole of creation" face.
Generously passed down by his mother and used sparingly.
The rest of the time he is an absolute sweetheart. And that's why you should be afraid.
He teaches Home Economics at a local high school. He is both loved and feared.
Elio De León
Alias: Hush
Abilities:
Versed in multiple fighting techniques and weapons. Prefers knives to guns.
Classified:
Assassin
Elio De León DOESN'T EXIST, in any official capacity. Except when someone needs to be killed, and there's a price tag attached. He is extremely lethal to his targets, but USUALLY exercises restraint against anyone he's not actually being paid to kill.
He'll still hurt them, though. If he feels so inclined.

CHARACTER SKETCHES

PAGE PROCESS

CHAPTER ONE, PAGE ONE

SKETCH

INKS

COLORS/LETTERS

MEREDITH MCCLAREN

is tired.

And clearly filthy.

When not safely atop her bed, cocooned in a burrito of comfort, she has worked on stories like *Hinges*, *Heart in a Box*, and *Hopeless Savages*. And also this one. That you are holding in your hands. Right now.

Possibly while also in bed.

You can find her website at:
meredithmcclaren.tumblr.com

Her Patreon at:
patreon.com/meredithmcclaren

And her Twitter at:
@IniquitousFish

But you might have to get out of bed to check those websites.

Best not risk it.

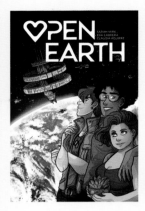

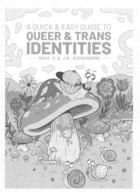